Muhammad
ALI

THE GREATEST

Muhammad
ALI
THE GREATEST

John Hennessey

PARKGATE
BOOKS

First published in 1999 by
PRC Publishing Ltd,
Kiln House, 210 New Kings Road, London SW6 4NZ

This edition published by
Parkgate Books
London House
Great Eastern Wharf
Parkgate Road
London SW11 4NQ
Great Britain

Reprinted 2000
Copyright © 1999 PRC Publishing Ltd

British Library Cataloguing in Publication Data:
A catalogue record for this book is available from the British Library.

ISBN 1 902616 64 2

Printed and bound in China

CONTENTS

the
GREATEST

MUHAMMAD ALI
THE FINEST, BRAVEST FIGHTING
MACHINE EVER, WAS BORN TO BE 'THE GREATEST.'
The handsome American brought the skills and speed of a lightweight into the heavyweight arena with refreshing brilliance, and made his opponents dance to his tune.

Previous page: A poet and a pounder — The Greatest in 1966.

Right: c. 1963, Cassius Clay kisses his mother near his father and brother at the Carlerton Hotel.

From the time he beat Polish veteran Zbigniew Piertrzkowski to win the 1960 Olympic light-heavyweight gold medal in Rome, Ali, then known as Cassius Clay, was destined for the top, destined to be something extra special. Though his involvement with Black Power leader Malcolm X and the Muslim faith caused him untold troubles in his early professional life, and his refusal to accept conscription for Vietnam almost cost him his career, Ali remained true to his beliefs and was, in time, recognized as the world's best-known man. Better known, perhaps, than the Pope or any American President! His 'Float like a Butterfly, Sting like a Bee' motto, inspired by faithful handler Bundini Brown, became a worldwide catch phrase, as did his 'I am The Greatest, I am The Prettiest' exhortations before, during and after his colorful boxing contests.

Derided as a frightened clown before his first world heavyweight challenge against the then awesome Sonny Liston, Cassius Clay appeared deranged at the weigh-in and doctors were alarmed at his blood pressure. An hour later, having laughed his head off behind the scenes, he was resting peacefully, his pulse back to normal. That night, 25 February 1964, Clay bamboozled nearly every boxing critic and expert by forcing a bewildered Liston to quit on his stool, supposedly with torn shoulder muscles, at the end of the sixth round. Clay, the perfectly proportioned new heavyweight titleholder, the second youngest in history behind Floyd Patterson, was to become Muhammad Ali, the black people's champion. And, even before the obligatory return match with Liston, the legend had begun. For the next decade and a half, apart from three-and-a-half barren years when he was counted out by the authorities, Ali thrilled millions around the world with his unbelievable multi-punch combinations and Fred Astaire footwork.

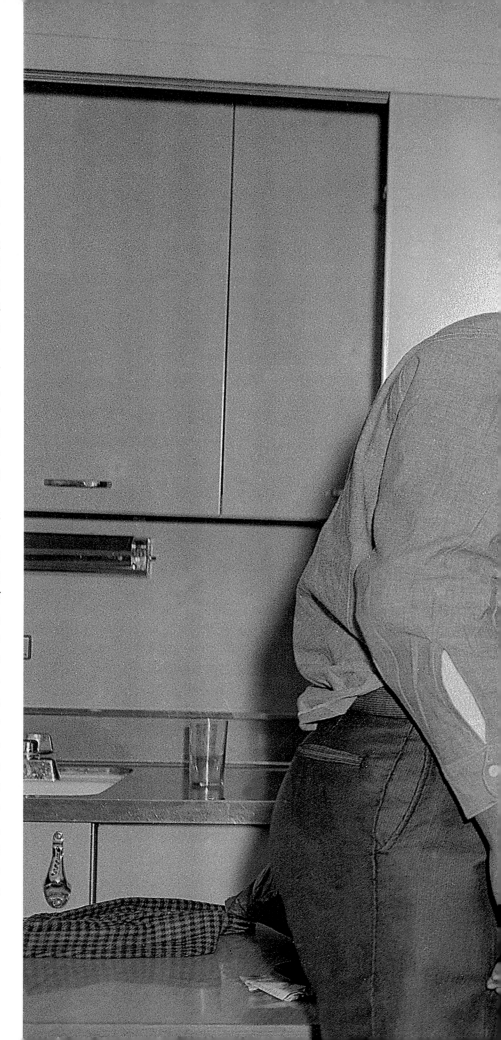

**Right: 'London here I come.'
Clay announces his fight with
Britain's Brian London. . . in
London. It was one of his easisi-
est defenses.**

**Far Right: 3 May, 1964. Posing
for the cameras in New York
City.**

Today, George Foreman says: 'Ali's the one who made it possible for us to earn such huge purses. To call him the greatest boxer of all time doesn't do him justice. He transcended boxing and inspired all athletes. He lifted baseball players, footballers and others, and inspired them to greater things.'

Some hated Ali's brashness but most forgave him because of the beauty he introduced to a brutal sport. Those who loved him wept tears of sadness when he lost for the first time in his career, against Joe Frazier for the undisputed heavyweight crown. They shed even more tears during his comeback when he broke his jaw in the second round against the tough Ken Norton but demonstrated his supreme courage by carrying on to the end only to suffer another defeat. Then came tears of joy when, on one of the most

momentous nights in heavyweight history, he destroyed the unbeaten monster George Foreman in what he labeled the 'Rumble in the jungle.' His third Frazier epic, the 'Thrilla in Manila,' overtook the Rumble for nerve-racking, pulse-quickening, raw excitement. Every fight fan marveled at the tenacity and courage of both fighters through 14 of the most ferocious rounds ever staged. Still Ali wouldn't call it a day after his two fiercest battles, and when he took the young Leon Spinks too lightly in 1978 he paid the price with defeat against a novice and we wept tears of incredulity.

Nine months on and slim, trim Ali was restored to the throne after a one-sided revenge points win against Spinks. He slid into retirement. . . and if only he'd stayed there. Having become the first man to

Right: Ali arrives in New York in 1964, with his wife, to train for the forthcoming fight with ex-champion Sonny Liston. He also has a date to pick up his championship belt from *Ring* magazine, even though the World Boxing Association had decided to strip him of his title.

regain the heavyweight crown on three separate occasions and accumulating untold wealth in the process, the great Ali was reduced to a stumbling, bumbling wreck. It was said he had the dreaded Parkinson's Disease, which ruthlessly attacks the nervous system.

At 38, he trimmed himself down to his proper fighting weight for the first time in years but, utterly weight-drained, the effort took its toll and he took a fearful yet merciful beating from Larry Holmes, once his sparring partner, in 1980 in Las Vegas. A washed-up Ali was retired on his stool at the end of the tenth

Left: 4 August, 1966. In training for the World Heavyweight title.

Right: 1966, London, England. Jimmy Brown, Cleveland Browns' ace back, joins the heavyweight champ in his morning roadwork.

Far Right: A portrait of Muhammad Ali, a proud warrior who loved the limelight.

round and Holmes became the first and only man ever to stop him. Even then the weary old man refused to quit, fighting the up-and-coming Trevor Berbick in the Bahamas and getting whipped over 10 one-sided rounds 13 months later. Only the vast army of hangers-on, the spongers who had lived the good life on his back for several years, pleaded with him to carry on.

The once-proud warrior who loved the limelight above all, who loved the glare of the spotlight as he entered the ring and loved the roar of the crowd chanting 'Ali, Ali, Ali,' finally saw the light. But it was too

Left: Muhammad Ali training at the Territorial Army Gymnasium in London, England, 1966.

Far Left: 14 January, 1965. Sammy Davis Jr., who played a boxer in the play *Golden Boy*, tries to get the attention of Ali during a visit backstage at the Majestic Theater in New York.

late. When he hung up his gloves forever late in 1981 his health was in shreds. Ali, the ultimate warrior, the wise-cracking genius who always seemed smart enough to crack the brutal system which had bled champions dry since men first squared up to each other to provide sport, had succumbed to his pride for too long. Who could possibly have foreseen such a tragic ending to the most dazzling career of all?

tomorrow's
CHAMPION

HIS TRAINING HAD
FINISHED FOR THE DAY AND
14-YEAR-OLD CASSIUS MARCELLUS CLAY

BATTLING ON HIS MOTORIZED SCOOTER AGAINST the rain, suddenly heard the roar of a crowd blaring from the radio of a parked car. What happened next almost certainly decided his destiny because he stopped, eager to know what was going on, and heard the announcement over the noise — 'And still heavyweight champion of the world, Rocky Marciano.' The youngster from Louisville, Kentucky, where blacks and whites were still segregated, had already harbored thoughts of becoming a pro boxer. And now, as he continued his journey, his dreams ran away with him — 'And still heavyweight champion of the world, Cassius Clay.'

He and Marciano were later to become good pals, but at the time Clay was a skinny kid, and hardly looked like filling out. More of a hurdle was the fact that he couldn't even beat some of the youngsters in his own gymnasium. But such was his desire to succeed that he became obsessed with winning, with being the best in his club to start with, then the best in his age group, and so on. The obsession led him to study in detail all the great fighters on TV and he drew encouragement from each one. Already Clay had discovered his ability to lean away from shots, to entice opponents to throw wasted punches, and he surmised that it was easier to avoid punches like that than to bob from side to side. His unique style, unparalleled in boxing history, was at the formative stage but he loved Sugar Ray Robinson, the fastest fighter in the world who had all the moves and, more especially, a stunning KO punch.

Training came easy to Clay. Because his family was poor, there was seldom enough money for Cassius and his big brother Rudy to take the bus to school each day. So Clay used to race it, pretending in part that he actually wanted to. He also used to measure up against the horses at the local racecourse when they were riding out each day. But even at that early age, despite a strict upbringing by his parents, he had become a boaster and was seen by some as an obnoxious big mouth. His trainer, Joe Martin, even threatened to pull him out of the Olympic trials at the semi-final stage if he didn't stop bragging following local newspaper criticism.

Once he'd achieved a degree of fame he was quickly labeled the 'Louisville Lip' by the Press. By that time it didn't matter though, because he could always be counted on to drum up publicity for his fights.

Ali discovered boxing by accident after his precious new bicycle, a Christmas present from his father, had been stolen. The distraught 12-year-old was told by a passer-by to report the theft to the local policeman, Joe Martin, who also ran the Columbia Gym. The smell of the gym and its surroundings captivated the boy, and after he saw Martin working as a corner man on TV during an amateur boxing show called 'Tomorrow's Champion,' he was hooked.

His first efforts were pitiful because he had no technique and, surprisingly, appeared to have little natural talent either. All he could do was thrash away with all his might in the hope that his opponents would succumb. They did. Within weeks, he had fought and won his first bout and inside a year he, too, was appearing on TV. Yet all he had to offer was raw courage until defeat by a classier opponent in the 'Golden Gloves' competition opened his eyes to the skill necessary to survive. Soon he was frequenting Fred Stoner's gym on the other side of town where his conqueror trained, much against Martin's wishes, and Ali insists he learned the finer points of the sport there. Stoner told him: 'You got the will but you don't have the skill.' That was to follow, rapidly, and Ali says in his colorful 1975 autobiography *The Greatest*: 'All the publicity about my boxing origins and the early development describes Joe Martin as the incubator. But my style, my stamina, my system were molded down in the basement of a church in East End, where Stoner ran his club.' At this early stage of his career, Clay was winning considerable support in his home town from frequent TV excursions, and he stirred up even more interest by promising to 'whip' his next opponent. 'I'd mouth off to anyone who'd listen about what I was going to do to anyone who fought me,' he recalled. 'I was only a kid fighter yet I was a drawing card because people would tune in hoping to see me beat.' His opponents were unlucky!

Once he'd developed his style there was no stopping him and his rise to fame in the amateur ranks, from lightweight through the divisions, was rapid. His

Previous Page: At 12-years-old Cassius Clay shows his best pugilist stance.

Left: 6 February, 1962. Cassius Clay, the Louisville slugger, a handsome 20-year-old, had been fighting since 29 October, 1960, and had won all of his ten fights — seven by knockout.

progress towards the Olympic team was inevitable after he had collected several state titles and the 1959 National 'Golden Gloves' and Amateur Athletic Union titles. Clay repeated the double in 1960. He truly was a golden boy with a glittering future. The AAU crown guaranteed him entry to the Olympic trials in San Francisco and at the tender age of 18 he was America's most experienced competitor. That didn't make him the most popular, though, because of his loud-mouth ways, but he smoothed his path to the final with a succession of victories.

Standing in his way of a place in the Rome Olympics was Army champion Allen Hudson, a vicious puncher who served notice of his intentions by decking Clay with a left hook in the first round. Clay held his own in the second round and in the third and final round, with the fight and his Olympic dream slipping away, the youngster suddenly found an opening. A right cross landed flush on Hudson's jaw and Clay followed up with a dazzling combination which was to become a trademark in the years to follow. The referee stopped the fight, despite Hudson's repeated protests, and Clay was on his way to Rome as the top amateur light-heavyweight in America.

Although Clay insists his main ring education came courtesy of Fred Roper, Martin was his corner man and both trainers were convinced he would win a gold medal. Martin was unable to accompany him to Rome, however, because of a family illness and so the bragging began in earnest again. With no one to calm him down, Clay quickly made himself unpopular in the Olympic village. His outlandish behavior attracted the bulk of media attention, which meant his team-mates were largely overshadowed.

But once again he served up the goods, stopping a Belgian, then outpointing a vastly-experienced Russian in his opening contests. Next on his list was Tony Madigan, the Australian who had inflicted on Clay his

Left: 1 September, 1960, Rome, Italy. Cassius Clay jolts Russian boxer Shatkov with a right to the head in their bout.

first defeat in the 'Golden Gloves.' This time Clay, his confidence sky-high, outsmarted him in a tough contest to reach the final. For all his boasting, Clay really was a polished performer and he proved it again in the final against Piertrzkowski when he battered the Polish champion in a spectacular third round to take the gold. 'I told you I am the greatest,' bellowed the brash youngster, proudly displaying his victor's medal around his neck.

Clay was given a hero's reception when he returned to Louisville and he was in big demand. An Olympic gold was, and still is, the best possible currency for a passport into the pro game and the big time. Martin had lined up a local millionaire businessman to be his manager but Cassius Clay Snr. didn't like the idea and his son was eventually handled by a wealthy 10-man Louisville consortium. They put up a $10,000 signing-on fee — a fortune for the Clay family — and were in return guaranteed 50 percent of his prize money for the six-year contract. It was to prove a magnificent financial investment.

Cassius Clay's entry into the professional ranks was an inauspicious affair. With Fred Stoner in the corner at his request, he plodded through a dreary six-round points win against unknown, unsung Tunny Husaker, a white nohoper heavyweight from Fayetteville in West Virginia. Clay displayed none of the punching power that had made him such a big hit in the Olympics and though he should have been pumped up to the limit on his pro debut, he seemed distinctly uninterested in the affair. The sponsoring group was not impressed, either with Clay or his trainer, and the youngster was soon dispatched to Archie Moore's training camp on the West Coast. Bill Faversham, who headed the group, felt the great old veteran could teach Clay the tricks of the trade because, despite his repertoire of skills, he was, basically, still a novice.

Right: In 1960, Clay was bigger and so was his reputation.

Clay, in fact, had already singled out Joe Louis to manage him — but the former heavyweight champion didn't like the young braggart. He also went for Sugar Ray Robinson, who had been a great source of inspiration to the youngster with his own quicksilver skills. Robinson, at the veteran stage of his fighting career, loved the flashy moves Clay demonstrated in front of him but felt it was too early to get involved, a decision he was later to regret. Then came the reunion which was to forge boxing's greatest partnership. Clay, fed up with the dull routines laid down at Moore's San Diego training camp, soon returned to Louisville and met with Angelo Dundee, former manager-coach of world light-middleweight champion Willie Pastrano. Dundee had an impeccable pedigree and the two men remembered each other well.

A few years earlier, a teenage Clay had pestered Dundee for an audience with then contender Pastrano, who was in Louisville for a fight. Clay angled his way up to their hotel bedroom then later sparred a round with him and wanted more, only for Dundee to call a halt.

Angelo undoubtedly liked what he saw, enjoyed the kid's style and loved his enthusiasm. Every time he turned up in Louisville with a fighter, there was Cassius, his brother Rudy and even his mum and dad to greet him. Soon Clay was getting free tickets for the fights. So there was an initial, mutual friendship upon which the two men could build when the subject of training Clay came up. Dundee's friends thought he was crazy to handle the youngster, who just couldn't stop talking about himself But Dundee understood Clay, understood what he was all about and wasn't surprised when the boy insisted on joining him in Miami Beach to prepare for a fight rather than be with the family for Christmas.

Clay settled into a routine at Dundee's gym, but he hated the fact that he couldn't box all the time. The wily Dundee was soon able to utilize the boy's strengths and weaknesses. Clay had to be the instigator, the initiator of all things. Of course, he wasn't, but Dundee allowed him to think he was. 'You can't improve on a fighter's natural ability,' he was to say. 'All I did was improve what he had and add a few wrinkles.' In other words, he allowed Clay to take all the credit for any adjustments that were made to his technique. It wasn't the done thing and it probably wasn't professional to act in this way, but Dundee knew Clay was something special and he was more than happy to improvise. Clay's first fight under Dundee came two days after Christmas at Miami Beach when he met Herb Siler on the undercard of a Willie Pastrano show. Clay KO'd him in four rounds and promptly bragged: 'I'm gonna be the heavyweight champion of the world.' It was to be a familiar message trumpeted after every victory from then on. His next two fights also ended in quick time, then the experienced Donnie Fleeman took him seven rounds before being stopped on cuts. Fleeman had won 45 of his 51 contests and was just the sort of opponent to push Clay. It was new territory for the kid and he handled the situation well. Next came a fight in his hometown, against Lamar Clark, another ring-wise fighter from Utah who boasted a big KO punch. He had seen off 45 opponents in this way but Clay, ever mindful of the publicity and his image, predicted he would sort him out in two rounds. Clay succeeded and, after thrashing his white rival, moved on to Las Vegas for his next bout, against Duke Sabedong. The glamor of the town, and the occasion, got to him, especially when he and Duke were being introduced on local TV. Even as they talked with the interviewer, they were upstaged by the outrageous wrestler 'Gorgeous George,' who had long flowing blond locks and a robe to match. Clay looked on in bewilderment as he took over the show, saying: 'I am the world's

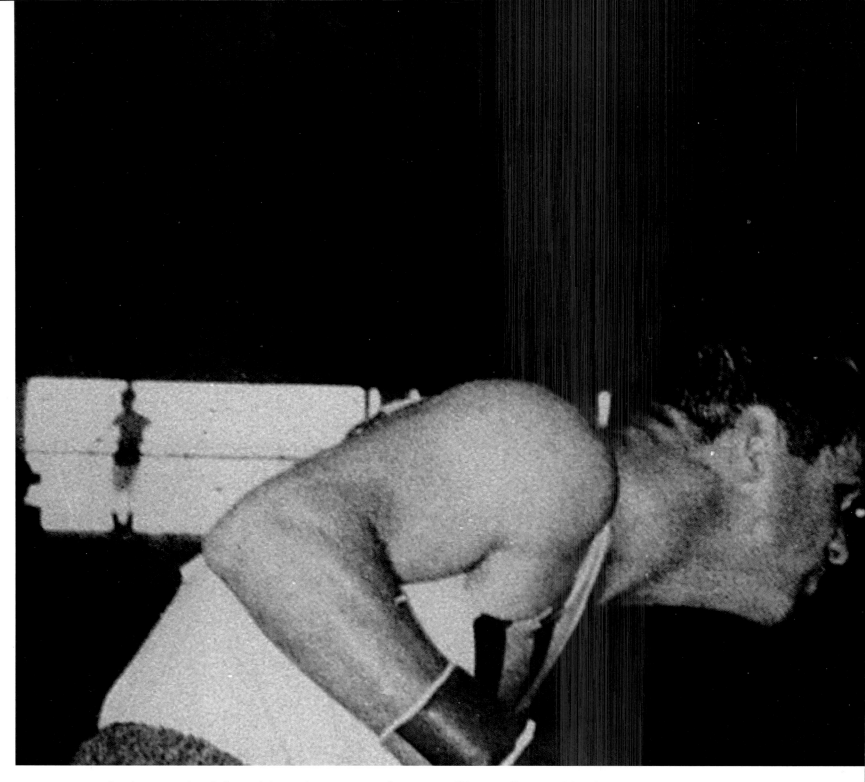

greatest wrestler. I cannot be defeated. I am the great-est. I am the king.'

Clay later recalled the incident, telling reporters that, 'Gorgeous George purred, "look at my velvet skin. Look at my pretty hair. If that bum messes my hair up tomorrow night I'll annihilate him. I want all of you out there to come to the Sports Palace early because I'm gonna mop the floor with this bum. If he beats me I'll cut off my golden hair and throw it out to the audience and go bald."'

Clay loved the colorful banter and sure enough he was there in the crowd to see Gorgeous George perform the following night. The crowd booed and jeered George, threw paper cups at him and derided him. But he won, as he always did. Just as Clay knew he, too, was destined to be a winner.

Left: 3 September, 1960, Rome, Italy. Cassius Clay throws a hard right at Australia's A. Madigan, during their light-heavyweight semi-final of the Olympic boxing tournament.

The seeds of greatness had been sown before then in Clay's own mind and the Gorgeous act was yet another factor he employed for recognition. Surprisingly, he took 10 laborious rounds to polish off Sabedong, but he was already dreaming of a world title shot. It seemed a ludicrous ambition since Sabedong, while a decent pro, was hardly a springboard for world dreams. But there was no holding him and his next test came against Alonzo Johnson, the first ranked opponent he had fought in his hometown Louisville. Again, Clay was taken the 10-round distance but this time he was much more assured, winning nearly every round and confirming that he was more than prepared to step up into the big time.

stepping
STONES

THE BRASH YOUNGSTER
HAD PROVED HIMSELF, IF NOT
TO FIGHT FANS, THEN CERTAINLY
TO DUNDEE, HIS MOST IMPORTANT CRITIC.
The battle-hardened trainer felt it was now time for a
major advance, but while he kept things strictly low
profile, Clay could not resist naming the round he
would win in advance... and getting it right so often
that it was hardly surprising he was receiving maxi-
mum publicity for one so raw. Alex Miteff was stopped
in six, as predicted, and Clay was right again when he
took Willie Besmanoff out in a round more.

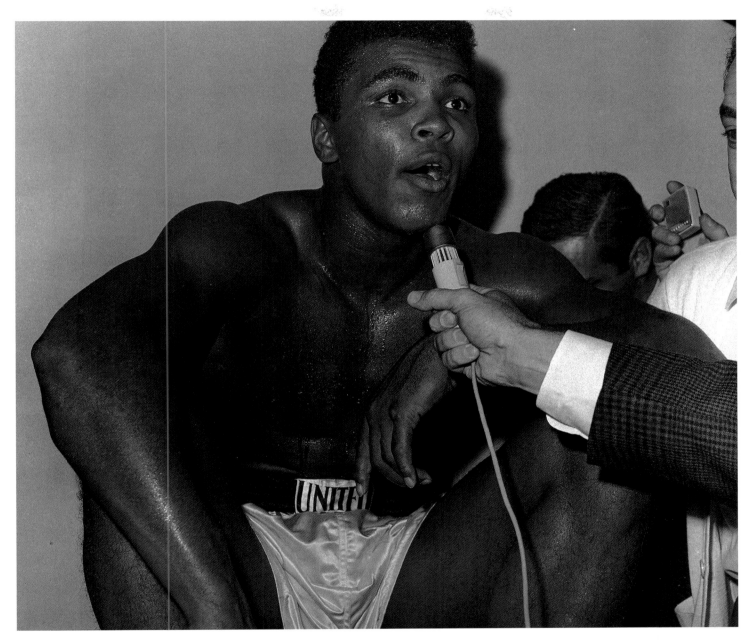

Previous Page: 28 February, 1962, Miami. Cassius Clay vs. Don Warner. Clay won by a knockout in the 4th round.

Left: 16 November, 1962. Cassius Clay talks to newsmen in his dressing room at the Los Angeles Sports Arena late after his heavyweight title elimination bout with Archie Moore. The 20-year-old youth KO'd his 45-year-old opponent in the fourth round as he had said he would.

Far Left: 15 November, 1962. Cassius Clay hits Archie Moore with a right to the side of he head in the first round.

Yet when he did step up a class, with venue and opponent, he very nearly came unstuck because of his cockiness. At short notice, Dundee matched him with another young prospect, Detroit's Sonny Banks, at New York's famed Madison Square Garden, home of American boxing, and Clay couldn't resist predicting: 'The man must fall in the round I call. Banks must fall in four.' It was corny, but the juvenile rhymes attract-

ed even more attention. All eyes were on Clay when he met Banks and for two rounds the script went according to plan as he danced rings around his opponent. But Banks shook him rigid in round three when he caught his clowning opponent with a left hook to the jaw.

He always maintained it was a slip, but either way he recovered his senses to fend Banks off for the

Right: 4 March, 1964. The boxer is interviewed by a reporter in front of the United Nations with his brother, Rudolph Valentino Clay, Black Muslim leader Malcolm X, and Nigerian ambassador to the UN S.O. Adebo.

remainder of the round. Then, as if to prove he really hadn't been tagged, Clay came out blazing in the appointed round and carried out his prediction.

Within months Clay had worked himself up to a confrontation with the veteran Archie Moore, whose methods he had shunned when he first turned pro. Moore, a great light-heavyweight champion at his prime, could no longer make the weight and, at 43 years of age — some say much older — this was a final fling for him. Moore reckoned he had developed a 'lip-buttoner' to shut Clay up, but in reality he was no match for the super-slick youngster, who again selected round four with another slushy rhyme that was to be his stock in trade over the years. Sure enough, after coasting through the early stages and flooring him, Clay opened up in the fourth and decked the old-timer again. Moore, still retaining his immense pride, managed to beat the count, but he couldn't beat a champion in the making, and the referee quickly intervened to rescue him. It was November 1962, just 25 months after he had first joined the paid ranks, and for the first time in his 16-fight career, Clay had received national exposure on TV. He had also earned a princely $45,000, his biggest purse, but a mere fraction of what lay ahead. It was the first genuine sign that he had what it took yet, oddly, the win didn't go down well with the fans, who booed him loudly for thrashing the legendary Moore.

Sonny Liston, the giant, brooding heavyweight champion who was at the ringside during the Banks' fight was Clay's next, seemingly improbable target. Though the youngster was now being taken seriously, no one outside his immediate close-knit circle could envisage feeding him to the lion. 'Liston in eight,' bragged a jubilant Clay afterward, but 'Old Stone Face,' as Liston had been dubbed, told Clay chillingly: 'You go eight seconds with me little boy and I'll give you the title.' Most of the media, amused at times by

Clay's ranting, would love to have seen Liston shut him up once and for all, but they were forced to wait as Clay marked time with a routine three-round win over Charlie Powell, an ex-gridiron footballer. While Liston prepared for a rematch with Floyd Patterson, the hapless world champion he had demolished to win the crown, Clay was being asked by his management for final proof of his credentials with a tough test at the Garden against world number two Doug Jones, who had moved up a division after campaigning for top honors as a light-heavy.

Jones was a Liston lookalike who joined the endless list of exceptional fighters who never managed to win a world title. Jones was tough, like Liston, could even punch like the champion, and he had something extra: unlike Liston, he was a smart fighter. Clay's vanity stopped him from believing anyone could be as smart as him and he underestimated Jones drastically. It almost proved his undoing. His pre-fight rantings failed to unnerve Jones, as they would later do Liston, and his extraordinary speed and skills also failed to ruffle him. Again the youngster predicted round four but Jones was far too good to be suckered and carried the fight to him. Round four came and went and Clay found himself on the receiving end of boos from the crowd. By round five he was being reminded forcefully that he was taking part in a 10-rounder and Jones began cutting back Clay's early lead as the fight went on.

By the ninth there was nothing in it and all that stood between them was guts, sheer guts. And Clay found them as he brought it back up from his boots in two final, stirring rounds to eke out a controversial if correct decision. According to many ringsiders Jones had just sneaked it, but the two judges had Clay winning by a round, while the referee gave it to him comfortably. The braggart had won again but to the sound of boos, yet he'd passed a severe examination of his talent and heart, and was later to demonstrate just how smart he was. As Muhammad Ali, he gave many fighters return matches throughout his career, but Jones was never given that option. Clay wasn't that stupid.

His stock had fallen somewhat with this display, yet Clay was in even bigger demand and, more to the point, a legitimate title challenger. But there was to be one final test before the inevitable showdown with big, bad Liston, who was being hailed as an invincible, cast-iron monster by the Press even before he had destroyed Patterson a second time. Britain's popular Henry Cooper, a cut-prone yet fearsome left-hooker, was the choice and Wembley the venue. For all Clay's bragging about what he would do to the 'tramp,' 'this bum' who would fall in five, many English fans warmed to the handsome American and his daily antics as he trained in Hyde Park. Though they obviously wanted their man to win, Clay proved to be a major attraction, although like many Yanks, there were thousands of Britons who wanted the balding Cooper to shut him up.

Trouble was, victory for Cooper — an improbability given his record — would not have pitched him in with Liston. Cooper's manager, friend and mentor Jim Wicks loved him like a son and had already insisted: 'I wouldn't let Henry in the same town as Liston, let alone the same ring.' Such was the interest that tickets sold out well in advance, but Clay wasn't interested. His mind was focused firmly on Liston, but his lack of respect for Cooper put him on that high-wire again and ultimately provided one of the great talking points of his entire career and an historic moment in British boxing history.

The outrageous Clay arrived at the weigh-in wearing a mock crown and ermine robe proclaiming: 'I'm the next king of boxing' and 'This ain't no jive, Cooper will fall in five.' But 29-year-old Cooper, roared on by

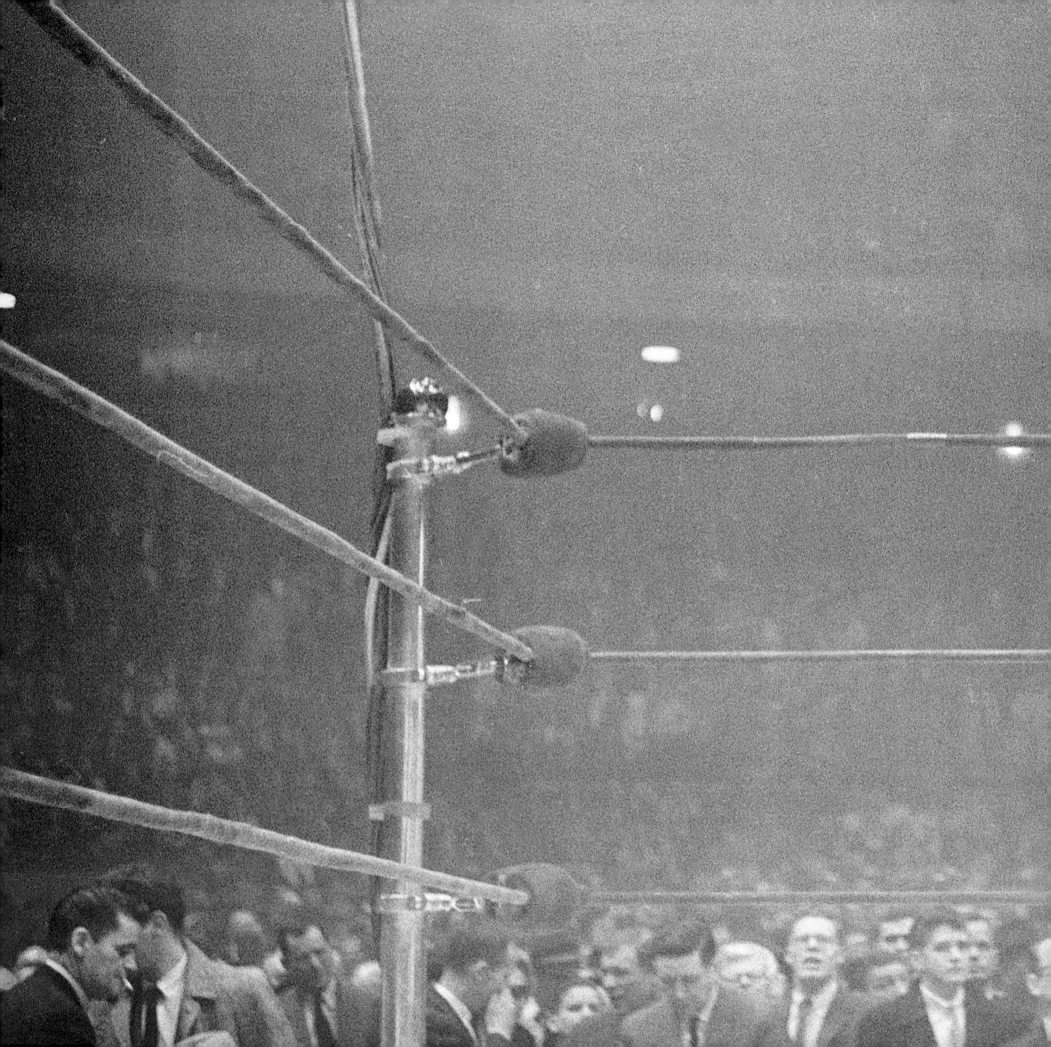

an army of devoted supporters, hadn't read the script. He surprised Clay with an early assault and kept up the pressure throughout round one without causing any real damage. He was relentless, whacking Clay on the break several times, but once the youngster found his range in the next round he began peppering his older opponent with snappy left jabs.

The crowd bayed for Clay's blood but, almost inevitably, what they got was Cooper's as a cut appeared over his left eye. By round three it looked pretty bad and a further cut had materialized over his other eye. The end looked near but Clay, keen to carry

Left: 18 June, 1963, London, England. Cassius Clay, bewildered by Henry Cooper's unexpected and ferocious opening attack, is pinned on the ropes in the first round of their heavyweight match at Wembley in London. Though Cooper kept up the assault and managed to put Clay down at the end of the fourth round, the American fulfilled his boast and won the fight in the fifth. The referee, Tommy Little, stopped the fight because of cuts over Cooper's eyes.

Far Left: 14 March, 1963, New York. A victorious Cassius Clay is joined in his dressing room by Sugar Ray Robinson and Cleveland Browns football star Jimmy Brown. Unbeaten Clay failed to knock out Doug Joes but his long-armed jabs and straight rights did win him an unpopular, unanimous 10-round decision in their heavyweight contenders' fight.

out his round five prediction, appeared to be coasting when Cooper forced him to the ropes and exploded a magnificent left hook against his jaw. 'Ennry's 'Ammer,' as it was called affectionately, had paid dividends as Clay crumpled against the ropes only to be saved by the bell. 'I was dazed and numb,' he admitted, but to be fair he was looking to his corner for guidance even as he lay on the canvas and we will never know how badly he was hurt. In following years he was to demonstrate his magnificent courage and will to survive time after time, and it is possible he would have been able to hang on and clear his head.

In the event, Dundee was taking no chances. As Clay wobbled back to his corner, his trainer noticed some padding sticking out of his glove. He quickly tore open the glove and insisted on a new pair, thus gaining Clay a valuable minute or so in which to recover. That was all he needed, and with Cooper masked with blood within seconds of the start of round five, referee Tommy Little did the only thing possible under the circumstances and stopped the fight. Even a relieved Clay acknowledged the seriousness of Cooper's condition and showed concern while his new pal Drew Bundini Brown pranced around the ring with the mock crown Clay had worn earlier. 'I'd have knocked him out,' said a disconsolate Cooper, while Clay, viewing the British champion with a new respect, admitted it was the hardest shot he'd ever taken.

Cooper was to be given another chance against his adversary, but on that occasion circumstances were entirely different, even though the outcome was much the same. Cooper, a respected ringside radio commentator today, cemented his claim to Britain's sporting roll of honor in that first encounter, while for Clay it proved to be the last title stepping stone. In the crowd at Wembley was Liston's adviser, Jack Nilon, who must have been convinced a Clay match would be a pushover for his man. 'He wants you,' he told a blood-spattered Clay afterwards. 'He says to drink your orange and your milk shakes and stay healthy. You've talked yourself into a heavyweight fight.' Clay and his handlers were ecstatic. It was time to go hunting.

He was only 21 with just 19 fights behind him, and Clay's pursuit of Liston and his world crown was greeted with a mixture of incredulity and disbelief by most observers. How on earth, they reasoned, could this lippy kid take on the monster who had just driven ex-champion Floyd. Patterson out of town in complete humiliation for the second time? Yet he set

Left: 8 January, 1964, Miami Beach. 'That ape is almost as ugly as Sonny,' says Cassius Clay, as he clowns around with a Ringling Brothers Circus clown dressed in a gorilla costume.

about his task in frenzied fashion, baiting 'The Big Bear' — his own nickname for Liston — at every given opportunity. 'He's too ugly and slow for someone as pretty as me,' screamed Clay as interest mounted throughout the world. Hardly an opponent had failed to be impressed and overawed by Liston, yet Clay derided him, even to the extent of buying a bus which he had painted in several colors. His signwriter father added the inscription 'World's Most Colorful Fighter: Cassius Clay' across one side with 'Liston is great but he'll fall in eight' on the other.

Not content with that, the youngster decided during a promotional crosscountry tour from Los Angeles to New York to call on Liston at his Denver home at 3am. A bemused Liston climbed out of bed to see what was going on and was met with a chorus of shouts from Clay and his pals. Eventually Clay and Co. were moved on by police, but Liston must surely have felt his young opponent was somewhat deranged.

The great Rocky Marciano, the only undefeated world champ in history, certainly thought so. He was convinced Clay was horribly short of experience against a man he classed as a 'brute.' 'It's hard to tell

Left: 22 January, 1964. The Beatles pose with the World Heavyweight title contender during a visit to one of his training sessions in Miami.

Below Left: This is a tale of the tape for the World Heavyweight Championship bout between champion Sonny Liston and contender Cassius Clay.

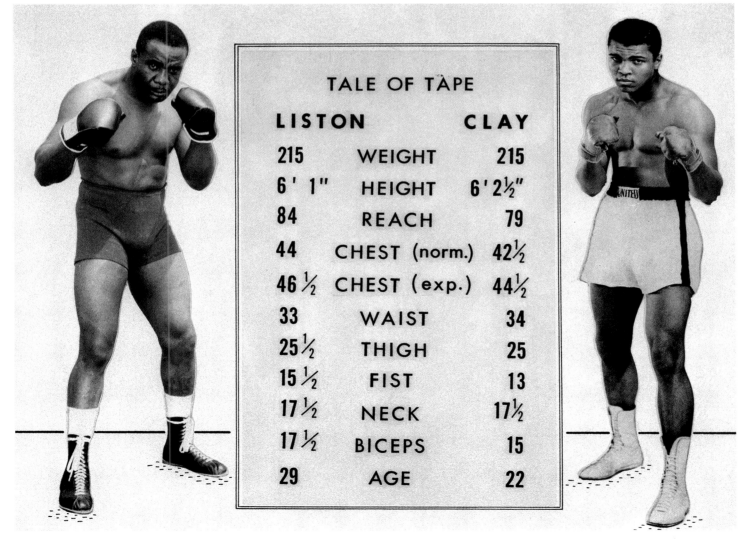

LISTON	TALE OF TAPE	CLAY
215	WEIGHT	215
6' 1"	HEIGHT	6' 2½"
84	REACH	79
44	CHEST (norm.)	42½
46½	CHEST (exp.)	44½
33	WAIST	34
25½	THIGH	25
15½	FIST	13
17½	NECK	17½
17½	BICEPS	15
29	AGE	22

Right: 17 December, 1964. Cassius Clay views the body of soul singer Sam Cooke at his wake in Chicago.

Below Right: 6 February, 1964, Miami Beach. Clay listens to trainers Angelo Dundee (Left) and Drew Brown, as he continues his 'psychological warfare' against Sonny Liston.

Far Right: Challenger Cassius Clay strains to break away from a friend who held him as he tried to lunge at champion Sonny Liston during weigh-in ceremonies. Clay was fined $2,500 for his antics by the Miami Beach Boxing Commission.

Clay not to fight this monster now, but I'm sure he'll be more receptive after he's been there with Liston,' said Marciano. Liston, who KO'd Patterson in two minutes ten seconds, referred to Clay as a 'fag' and added: 'If they ever make the fight I'll be locked up for murder.' But make it they did with Clay receiving a purse of nearly $500,000, enormous for a challenger but, after all, he was the star attraction.

The two men met face to face for the first time on 5 November, 1963, to sign for the fight. 'He's an old man,' said Clay afterwards. 'I'll give him talking lessons and boxing lessons.' The 'talking lessons' continued throughout the build-up to their 25 February 1964 confrontation in Miami then Clay appeared to flip his lid completely at the weigh-in. With 'Bear Hunting' emblazoned across his denim jacket, he stunned a

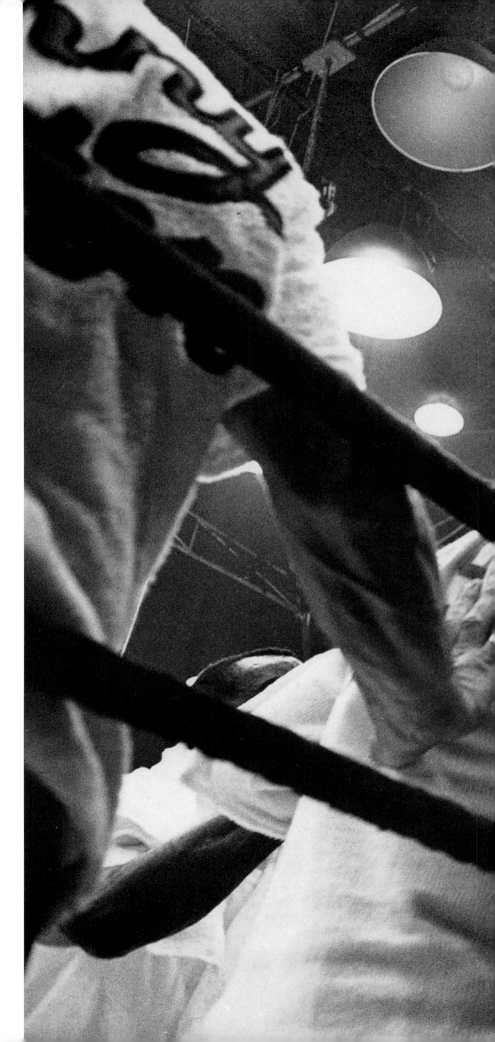

Right: Jubilation in the Cassius Clay camp after he defeats Sonny Liston to become the World Heavyweight Champion.

huge crowd of reporters with an unprecedented outburst. Flanked by his idol, Sugar Ray Robinson, and the faithful Bundini Brown, he screamed: 'You can tell Sonny I'm here with Sugar Ray. Liston is flat-footed but me and Sugar Ray are two pretty dancers. . . round eight to prove I'm great.' Then came his 'float like a butterfly, sting like a bee' routine with Bundini.

When Liston and his party slid quietly into the Convention Hall, Clay pretended to charge the champion, with Bundini holding him back. His pulse rate, normally 54 beats a minute, had more than doubled by the actual weigh-in and a concerned Dr. Alexander, who had just checked it, said: 'Clay is nervous and scared to death.' The sideshow hotted up still further when Liston stepped off the scale as Clay told him hysterically: 'You are too ugly. You are a bear, I'm going to whup you so bad.' Liston stood there impassively taking it all in. . . but had he fallen for the greatest act of young Clay's life? He was used to intimidating opponents with his cold stare and really didn't know how to handle the crazy kid. An hour later, as Clay rested in his hotel room, his personal doctor Ferdie Pacheco was astonished to find his pulse rate back to normal.

The fight drew an 8,000-plus crowd with 10 times that number watching worldwide in cinemas, but few felt they would see more than a round or so. Clay was rated a 7-1 underdog with no betting on Liston. It was a formality, said the experts. But they and Liston were shocked from the first bell. Liston shambled forward, threw his regular, punishing left jab, and it missed by miles. The grin on Clay's face was as wide as a slice of melon as he made the champion miss time and again. By the middle of the second round Liston was beginning to be rocked back by Clay's snappy left jabs … and he didn't like it. This wasn't boxing as far as the champ was concerned, and he could find no solution to the twinkle-toed genius in front of him.

Right: Cassius Clay vs. Sonny
Liston, 1964.

Far Right: 25 February, 1964.
Cassius Clay, new Heavyweight
Champion of the world, raises
his arms in victory after Sonny
Liston failed to answer the bell
for the seventh round.

Then, toward the end of the third, Clay opened up
with a combination and a nasty cut materialized under
Liston's left eye. The doubters had begun to believe
this astonishing young fighter, but there was another
dramatic twist in the tale. Clay, comfortably in charge,
came back at the end of the fourth round complain-
ing that he couldn't see. Linament from Liston's cut
had somehow worked its way into his eyes and Clay
was convinced he was going blind. 'Cut the gloves off!'
he shrieked at Dundee, but his trainer ignored him
and pushed him out just as referee Barney Felix was
moving toward the corner to see what the commo-
tion was about.

Clay somehow danced his way through round five,
his eyes clearing every second, and in the sixth he cut
loose with a barrage of punches which made an old

man of Liston. There was nowhere for him to hide and
the brash challenger knew he had him. But there was
no hint of the sensation to follow. As the bell rang for
the seventh a dull-eyed Liston remained rooted to his
stool. The monster had been slain and the world salut-
ed boxing's greatest victory.

Clay embraced Dundee and Bundini, then ran
around the ring hollering: 'I told you I am greatest.'
Liston later complained of torn shoulder muscles but
the truth was that he really had been whupped, just as
the new champion predicted he would be. Clay had
blown up a storm in the ring, even though the
'experts' still felt it was a fluke result. He was about to
create another, more powerful one on the other side
of the ropes, the repercussions of which would
reverberate around the world for the next five

Far Left: 19 April, 1964.
Admiring boys surround
Muhammad Ali during an
appearance in the Roxbury
section of Boston where Ali
spoke to a Black Muslim
congregation.

Left: 7 March, 1964. Olympic
medal dangling from his neck,
Ali comes home to Louisville.
His mother, Odessa, embraces
him. His father (Right) and
younger brother, Rudolph
Valentino Clay, wait to congrat-
ulate him.

years. An increasingly regular visitor to Clay's training camp before the fight was Malcolm X, a black Muslim who had befriended the fighter. And less than 24 hours after his sensational win, Clay renounced his Christian faith in favor of the Islamic religion. Having spent his childhood in the Baptist church, Clay was now a dedicated Muslim, and along with his new faith came a new name, Cassius X to start with, then Muhammad Ali.

Immediately, it lost him all the admirers he had gained by beating Liston because the black Muslims were seen as an anti-American militant group, a

violent outfit said to hate whites. This added even more spice to the obligatory rematch but two unforseen events things happened before that could take place. First, the young champion married Sonja Roi and took her on tour to Africa, where he was hailed as a hero. Then, three days before the 16

November fight, Clay, or Ali as he now insisted on being called, was rushed to hospital with an acute hernia.

Fifteen long months were to pass from the original fight to the return, but on 25 May, 1965, the two men came together in Maine, with former champion Jersey

Left: 25 May, 1965. Ali stands over Sonny Liston and taunts him to get up during their title fight. Liston was knocked out in two minutes during the first round.

Joe Walcott in charge. The outcome was again sensational, this time Liston falling to a mystery Ali blow to the side of the head after just two minutes. Cries of 'fix' rang around the hall but Ali remained champion of the world. The arguments raged long and loud for months, the most popular theory being that Liston was almost frightened to death of his opponent and was looking to get the fight over with as soon as possible rather than risk a second humiliation. Ali claimed he had invented the corkscrew, punch which felled the beast, but he had a big grin on his face as he explained the KO. Already he was the most fascinating

Right: 27 May, 1965. A dramatic overheard photo reveals Sonny Liston spread-eagled on the canvas as Muhammad Ali raises his arms in triumph after two minutes of the first round of their title bout. The bizarre battle immediately triggered nationwide demands for a probe of the fight itself and a demand for federal control of boxing.

Far Right: 1 February, 1965, New York. Heavyweight Champion Muhammad Ali congratulates former champion Floyd Patterson, following the latter's victory over Canadian George Chuvalo at Madison Square Garden. Patterson won a unanimous decision over Chuvalo in the elimination bout.

sportsman in the world, but Ali's religious connections acted against him in America. Floyd Patterson, a Roman Catholic and the youngest champion ever, issued a challenge saying he wanted to bring the title 'back to America.' Ali responded by calling his fellow negro a 'Great White Hope' and vowed to cause him serious physical harm.

Having lost and regained his crown against Ingemar Johansson, then losing it to Liston, Patterson was attempting to be a three-time winner. But he had no

chance against the great Ali when they met on 22 November 1965 in Las Vegas. Ali labeled his opponent 'The Rabbit' and the insults began in earnest. When the fight started Ali refused to throw a worthwhile punch in the first round, making Patterson miss at every opportunity. In the third Patterson sustained a back injury and from then on he was tortured systematically by a callous champion until the referee finally showed mercy in the twelfth round. Patterson was said to have a glass jaw, yet Ali

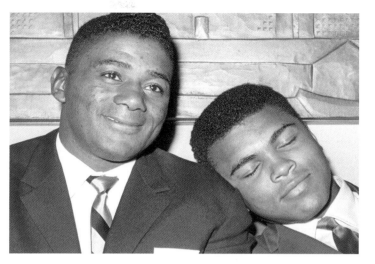

wasn't able to put him away throughout the one-sided contest.

Three months later Ali, having previously failed his Army induction exam, was reassessed as being fit for duty in Vietnam after the pass mark had been lowered. His response was to say war was against his new beliefs and added: 'I ain't got no quarrel with the Viet Cong. They ain't called me a nigger.' The statement enraged white America and again Ali, now managed by the shrewd Muslim Herbert Muhammad, found himself an outcast. He had been stripped of his title by the World Boxing Association and was due to meet Ernie Terrell, a tall, black fighter who had been put up as the WBA champion. But after virtually every American state refused the fight, Terrell pulled out.

Ali was forced to defend his title on foreign soil — albeit only across the border in Canada — and his new opponent was the rough, tough, clumsy George Chuvalo, who managed to last the full 15 rounds. Two months later, in May 1966, Ali flew to London for a rematch with Henry Cooper at Highbury Stadium, home of Arsenal Football Club. This time there were no dramas. Cooper, bleeding profusely from cuts, was retired inside six rounds without ever looking capable of knocking over his young rival again. By now the British public and Press had taken Ali to their hearts

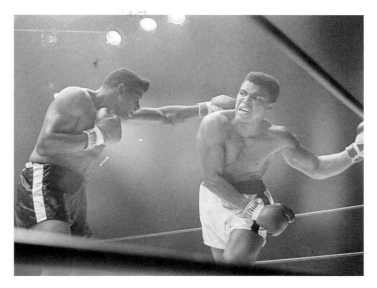

and he returned the same summer to administer a three-round beating to former British champion Brian London, who was hopelessly outclassed. With the draft call-up due at any time, Ali went to Germany a month later to fight their champion Karl Mildenberger, a southpaw who set him all sorts of problems until the twelfth round, when he crumbled.

That just about cleaned up the European scene for Ali and he returned to the States for a match with Cleveland Williams, who had troubled Liston a few years earlier. But Williams was no match for Ali, who displayed his most dazzling form since becoming champion to halt him in three rounds. Ali moved on to the unification showdown with Terrell at Houston's Astrodome where, cruelly, in front of some 37,000 fans, he tormented him for fully 15 rounds, asking repeatedly: 'What's my name, what's my name?' But the draft was closing in on Ali. A month later he met the veteran Zora Folley, a top contender for a decade, and retired him in seven painful rounds. It was to be his last fight for three-and-a-half years because three weeks later he refused to accept his induction. He was an outcast.

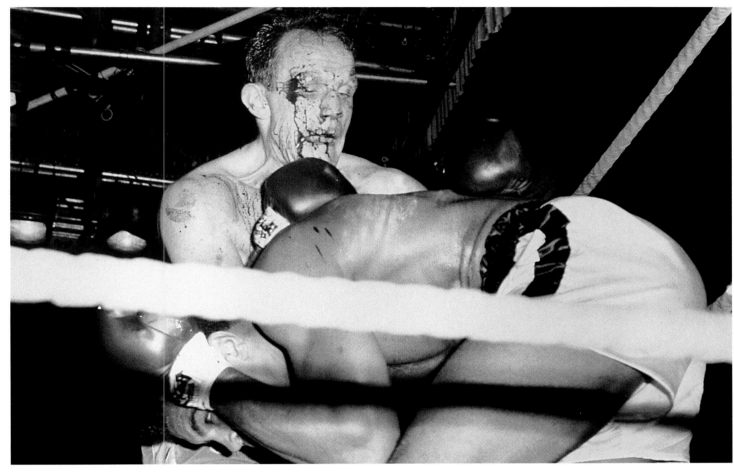

Far Left: 25 November, 1965.
World Heavyweight bout:
Patterson vs. Ali.

Left: 21 May, 1966, London.
World Heavyweight title: Henry
Cooper vs. Muhammad Ali.

Below Left: 6 August, 1966.
World Heavyweight bout: Brian
London vs. Muhammad Ali.

**Right: 10 September, 1966,
Frankfurt, Germany.
Muhammad Ali beats contender
Karl Mildenberger for the world
title.**

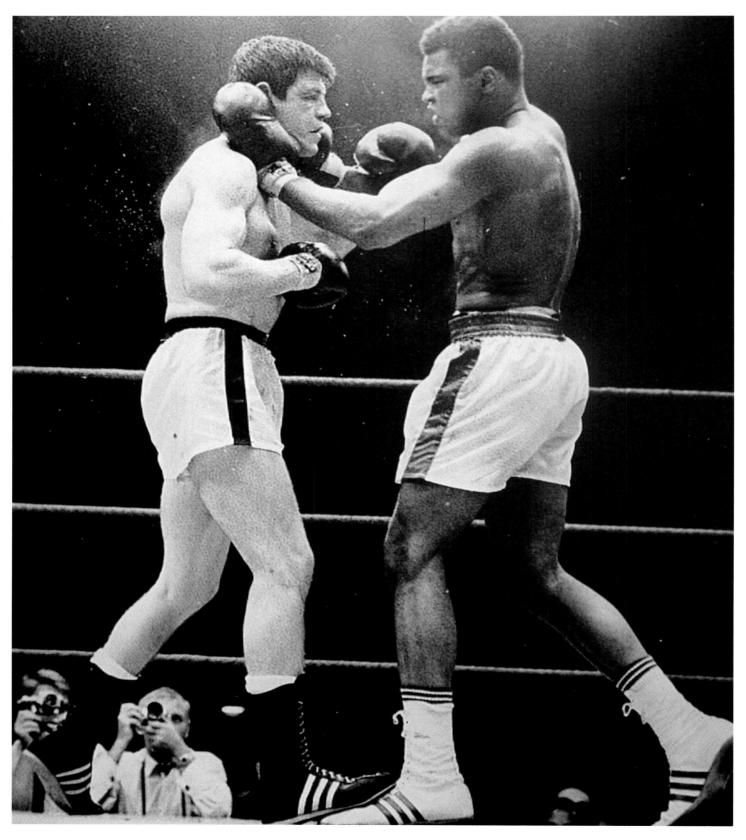

**Left: 14 November, 1966,
Houston. While challenger
Cleveland Williams lies
sprawled on the canvas, Ali
raises his arms in victory.**

Right: 6 February, 1967. Ali punches challenger Ernie Terrell in the third round of their Heavyweight Championship fight at Houston's Astrodome.

Left: 22 March, 1967, New York. Ali stands over the fallen challenger Zora Folley in the 7th round of their title bout at Madison Square Garden.

the
OUTCAST

'I SAID I WAS THE GREATEST NOT THE SMARTEST,' WAS ALI'S RESPONSE TO THE NEWS THAT HE had failed two draft tests. As an 18-year-old he had registered for the armed forces shortly before the 1960 Olympics but, as he later argued in his defense: 'I was a Christian then and knew nothing about Islam and had I been drafted then I would have gone.' When, predictably, Ali refused induction in April 1967, he was just 25 years old, at his absolute prime, and destined for his toughest fight — against the US Government.

He was fined $10,000 and given a five-year prison sentence, suspended on appeal. American whites called him a coward 'nigger scum' and directed even worse derogatory remarks toward him. Both the Army and his sponsoring group attempted to convince him he wouldn't actually be involved in warfare, that he would spend his time giving exhibitions for the troops and generally bolstering morale. But he wouldn't have anything to do with their pleas. 'We did it for Joe Louis,' an Army chief reassured him. 'Yea, and look where he is now,' replied Ali, mindful that the old champ had fallen on hard times. 'Clay Hated By Millions' read one headline, and some ex-champs went on record as saying he was a disgrace to the country and the sport.

To complete his humiliation, Ali was also stripped of his title and the World Boxing Association instigated a series of eliminators to determine a new champion. Ali insisted: 'Everyone knows who the real champ is regardless of who wins,' but business is business and the fact remained that he was in the wilderness. So, too, was Liston but for other reasons. He wasn't even invited to take part because months earlier he had

Previous Page: Muhammad Ali addresses a Black Muslim Annual Convention.

Left: 27 April, 1967, Houston. Surrounded by newsmen and admirers, Ali looks skyward as he leaves Federal court in Houston, after a federal judge tossed out his last legal effort to avoid being drafted into the Army.

Below Left: 21 March, 1967, New York. The Madison Square Garden marquee shows the last advertising of a heavyweight championship fight at the Garden before the future bouts shift to the new Madison Square Garden later in 1967.

**Right: 5 April, 1967, New York.
Floyd Patterson and
Muhammad Ali make a
handsome picture as the
two sluggers sign to meet
for the World Heavyweight
Championship that Ali holds
and that Patterson once held.**

**Far Right: February 1968.
Muhammed Ali gestures
characteristically as he talks
to a crowd of some 1,500
students at California State
stadium. Ali remarked that
violence in the streets would
not aid the Negros' cause
and remarked, 'Rioting in the
ghettos is like a bull running
into a locomotive.'**

been KO'd sensationally by Leotis Martin in nine rounds. Liston, who was alleged to have underworld connections, was later found shot dead in his apartment. Joe Frazier, best of the prospects not to have fought Ali so far, refused to participate. Instead, as the title was carved up, he won another version and later went on to claim the overall crown. Jimmy Ellis,

former junior clubmate of Ali's in Louisville, beat white hope Jerry Quarry — later to figure prominently in Ali's comeback — to claim the WBA title, then defended against Patterson. Ellis was then stopped in four rounds by Frazier in a unification match.

Meanwhile, Ali's lawyers worked night and day without success to get his boxing licence reinstated,

as well as pressuring the government to rescind the sentence. Every knock-back, however, saw a new cloud of depression descend on the already dispirited ex-champ, who entertained serious thoughts of quitting the sport which had been his life. What lifted the cloud and rescued him to an extent was the new feeling of futility among American whites and blacks alike as the Vietnam war dragged on senselessly, cutting the country's lifeblood down in their prime. Suddenly, Ali was no longer an outcast, especially among the young people. In fact, he was a hero again and he began to earn a living of sorts on a nationwide tour of colleges. He also preached on the virtues of Islam.

Sadly, his new religious views clashed head-on with those of his wife and, as she grew weary of Ali's demands that she conform, the marriage crumbled after less than a year. Within months of exile, however, a new Mrs. Ali appeared. She was a pretty

teenager called Belinda who had been born into the Muslim faith and practised her religion devoutly. She was an ideal soul-mate for Ali and she was to bear him four children, including twin daughters, in the next five years.

Though Ali's finances had dwindled to zero, boxing had also paid the price for his absence because there were no readymade crowd-pullers and this brought an end to the big pay-days promoters had enjoyed with him. For all the furore he had caused by his religious and military declarations promoters were working side by side with his lawyers to get him back in the ring. They reasoned, correctly, that a showdown against Frazier — two unbeaten champions — would he the biggest selling fight of all time. But for all their effort in several states as the Sixties drew to a conclusion, they were thwarted by the respective authorities at every turn.

Left: 30 December 1970, New York. Each claiming to be the true champion, Muhammad Ali and Joe Frazier, the recognized heavyweight title holder, engage in a shouting match during a contract signing ceremony. The two agreed to meet on 8 March at Madison Square Garden to settle the matter in a bout that was assured of being the richest one-shot sporting event in history.

Both Ali and Frazier knew how much they needed each other; Frazier because there was no mammoth pay-day in the offing otherwise, and Ali to re-establish himself as the world's greatest. He was hardly rolling in money, anyway, with an ex-wife to support as well as his costly day-to-day finances. Publicly, Ali derided Smokin' Joe and privately, Frazier hated him, hated his slick way with words and vowed to button his lip once and for all. A good many other fighters had attempted the same but Frazier was different. The ex-slaughterhouseman from Philadelphia was fired up as never before because of the taunts. Yet for all the vitriol that flowed, there was much mutual respect between Frazier and Ali, who once in desperation even offered his services to the champion as a hired sparring partner for a few hundred dollars. But both were unbeaten and both knew there would be far more than a fistful of dollars at stake if they ever met in the ring.

Three barren years went by for Ali before the breakthrough came, first in June 1970 when his prison sentence was reversed, then three months later in Atlanta, Georgia, whose Mayor, Sam Massell, granted him a boxing licence. The Mayor was persuaded by Senator Leroy Johnson, the first black man ever to be elected in the Deep South — that it would be a good thing for the city, even though the state of Georgia had previously rejected an application. Johnson even joined the promotional team responsible for drumming up publicity. Not that any was needed. There was only one small snag: Frazier. Smokin' Joe, who saw himself as something of a soul singer, had gone on tour with his band and was in no condition to face Ali, ring-rusty or not. There was a solution, though, in the shape of Jerry Quarry, the talented Irish-American white fighter who was also a top contender. In fact, a black versus white contest in Atlanta, a predominantly black city, served only to add spice to the momentous occasion.

But could Ali really turn the clock back and recapture the dazzling brilliance with which he had illuminated the heavyweight division as no other before him? He certainly looked the part in training and sparring. Any surplus weight had been stripped off and his speed of foot and hand was still there. But the answer, on an incredible night in Atlanta, was not that easy coming.

Quarry could bang, of that there was no doubt, and he was always active, but could he really spoil Ali's big day and stage one of the greatest upsets in heavyweight history?

Along with such black ringside celebrities as Diana Ross, Sidney Poitier and Bill Cosby, part if not the full answer came on 26 October, 1970, as Ali climbed through the ropes for his first taste of serious action in 42 months. A sell-out crowd of thousands greeted his arrival ecstatically, and with closed-circuit TV ready to monitor his every punch, Ali was well and truly back in the spotlight. Such was the din that Ali's name could not be heard as the fighters were introduced, and it was almost as overpowering as Ali waded into Quarry from the first bell, whipping out combinations and jabs just like the old days. But it certainly wasn't like the old days in round two as an already wearying Ali slowed the tempo. Quarry, one of the best counter-punchers around, started catching him as his confidence grew and he finished the round well on top.

Ali's lack of serious ringwork showed, yet he came out as if rejuvenated in round three and caught Quarry with a flurry of punches. Blood began pouring from a cut over his opponent's eye, which encouraged Ali to step up an already cracking pace. At the end of the round Quarry trudged back to his corner as if knowing his night's work had been cut short. It had.

Left: January, 1971, New York.
A photographic portrait of
Muhammad Ali in action.

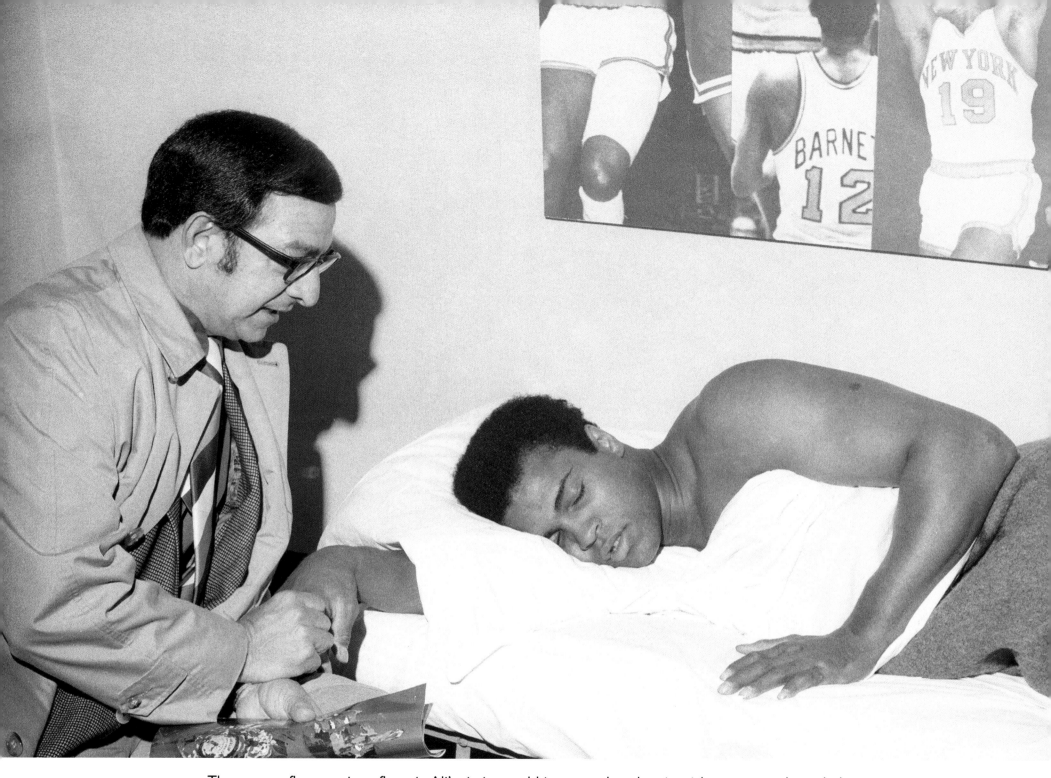

There were flaws, serious flaws in Ali's timing, and his legendary speed simply wasn't there for periods. 'I'm shocked that I was so tired,' admitted Ali, but had he really deteriorated that much or, was he simply shrugging off the lethargy which had overcome the greatest fighting machine ever assembled?

In fairness, Ali had been under immense pressure, and not just with his ring return. His wife Belinda had produced twin girls prematurely and there was no guarantee they would survive. She had already lost a son, who lived for only a few minutes, so there was additional cause for concern. Also, he and Bundini maintained they were shot at one morning in Atlanta while they were putting the finishing touches to his training. Ali also said he had received threatening phone calls warning him not to fight Quarry. For all

whether his deterioration was permanent before tackling Frazier.

They couldn't have chosen a tougher examination than Oscar Bonavena, the rough-and-tumble, chunk-of-muscle Argentinian with long Samson-like locks who fought with elbows, head and any other part of his anatomy that served as a weapon. He was as horrible as he looked and was married to a hooker. He would later die in a street brawl.

'If I can't beat him, I'm not ready for Joe,' said Ali, while the Frazier camp were convinced he was tossing away a fortune for both fighters. After all, Bonavena had decked Frazier twice in their first fight and gone the distance twice with the unbeaten champion, giving him the hardest scraps of his life. But Ali was adamant and for a near-$1 million purse, he took on Bonavena at New York's Madison Square Garden on 7 December the same year.

He nearly lived to regret it as the uncompromising Argentinian with the cast-iron jaw handled everything Ali threw at him and staged a late, dangerous rally that could have been conclusive. Unfortunately for him, Ali again dug deep into his resources in the fifteenth round and became the first man to KO Bonavena. Now for Frazier, but was Ali being premature? Surely he needed another warm-up fight or two to fine-tune his body? It was not to be. Exactly three months later, back at the Garden in front of another sell-out crowd, the two warriors settled their differences in a showdown billed as 'The Greatest Fight of the Century.'

Ali's last-round success over Bonavena and the manner in which he achieved it convinced him he could take Frazier at any time. After all, he'd beaten the time barrier and, anyway, he had the supreme conviction that he was invincible. But Frazier had the same unquenchable lust for greatness, he also yearned to be overall heavyweight supremo.

his popularity, he was still seen as a 'draft-dodging nigger' in some quarters. There were even death threats but, happily, they amounted to nothing and Belinda called before the fight to say she was back at their Philadelphia home with the twins. There was further good news when the state of New York also granted him a boxing licence. He was back in business but, for all that, Dundee and Ali still had to find out

Right: 19 July 1972, Dublin, Ireland. Muhammad Ali celebrates his win over Al 'Blue' Lewis, an 11th round stoppage.

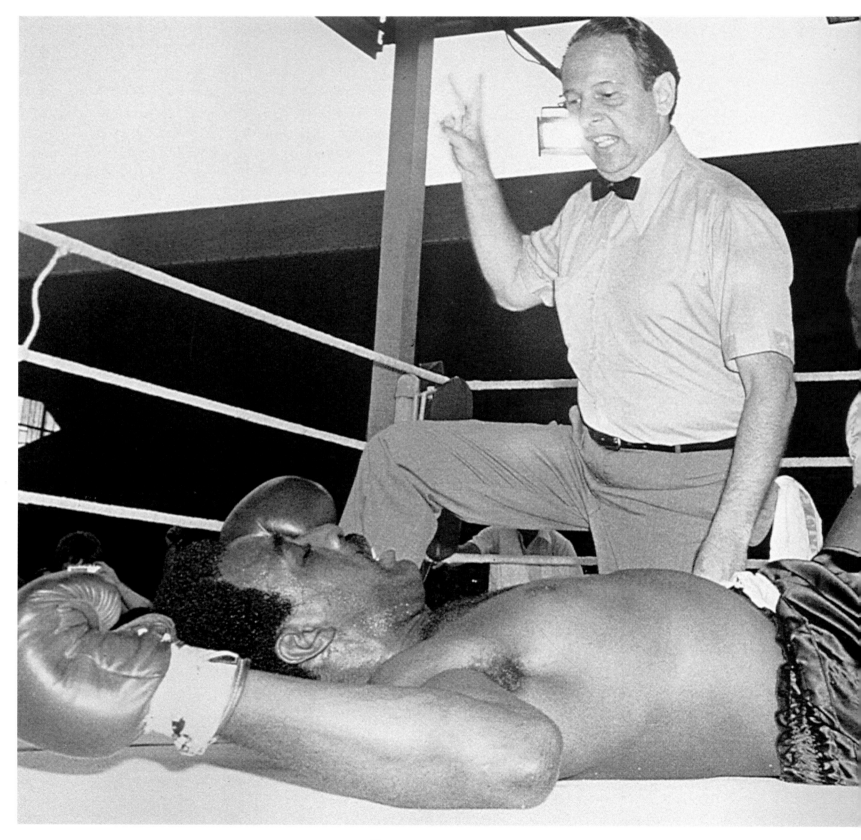

It really did have all the makings of a classic event — and the two undefeated champions obliged. Tickets for the Garden were sold out weeks in advance and a 25,000 crowd paid over $1,300,000, a record. Celebrities abounded throughout the arena, transforming the night into a glittering showbiz event. For the first time Ali topped the $1 million prize mark and Frazier, who had never been able to draw big money, was on the same $2,500,000 deal. But once they got to work the cash was far from their minds. Ali, with an eye to enhancing his own legendary status, knew he needed a great opponent, a Mount Everest to conquer, just as he did when he took the title from Liston. Joe Louis had his Schmeling, Robinson had his Basilio. . . and Ali had his Frazier.

But Frazier the gunslinger was oblivious to legends. He hated all that Ali stood for and his loathing, his burning desire to muzzle the Louisville Lip was ultimately his undoing. Smokin' Joe was born to fight. Reared in South Carolina, he packed his bags as a teenager in search of the big-time and headed for Philadelphia, home of the world's toughest fighters. Everything was geared around punishing nightly training sessions, and Frazier responded admirably, even at that early age. He took the first job he stumbled across — in a slaughterhouse — to cover his rent and gym fees, and legend has it that he actually killed some animals with his bare hands to stay in trim. By 1963 he was America's most feared amateur heavyweight and the following year in Tokyo he joined the Ali set by winning an Olympic gold. On his return he turned pro under the lovable, loyal Yancey 'Yank' Durham and soon punched his way into the top 10. His progress to the top, in the absence of Ali, was as inevitable as their clash at Madison Square Garden.

A full description of the fight would fill a book, such was its brutality and, perversely, its beauty. Frazier forced the fight from the off and early on it seemed obvious that Ali had seriously under-estimated his sawn-off opponent. His answer to Frazier's relentless pressure was to shake his head and wave to ringsiders. True, he was feeling the effects of the lay-off, but even the 1967 super-slick model would have had major problems keeping at bay an opponent who appeared possessed.

By round 10 Ali knew it was not to be his night. He towered over Frazier but Smokin' Joe, sniffing and snorting like a bull, also fought like one and there was nothing Ali could do to hold him back. Frazier bled profusely, he grimaced, he stopped occasionally to take in huge gulps of smoky air. But he never stopped coming forward, never stopped ramming everything in sight as his pistonlike fists slammed into every part of Ali arms, kidneys, thighs, neck. They were all the same to Joe, and the fight was slipping away from The Greatest.

The speed and sharpness had long left his limbs and Ali had run out of ideas by the last round. Even so, there wasn't much to choose between them. Then Frazier settled all arguments in round 15 of this titanic battle. He felt a tingle go down his arm as he caught Ali flush on the jaw with his pet left hook. Ali crumbled to the canvas, backside first, and it was a miracle he was even able to get up, let alone survive those last torrid seconds. The showdown was over and even the most committed Ali fans could hardly argue as the two judges and the referee gave the fight to Frazier unanimously. Yet it was Smokin' Joe who spent the next week in hospital recovering from his exertions, while Ali, bruised, battered and forlorn, did his best to recover his pride.

'I've never fought anyone with a will so strong,' he admitted. 'His face was a mass of blood and lumps, swollen, but so was mine. My jaw was swollen like a melon and my hips felt as though they'd been beaten by baseball bats.' There were few recriminations, how-

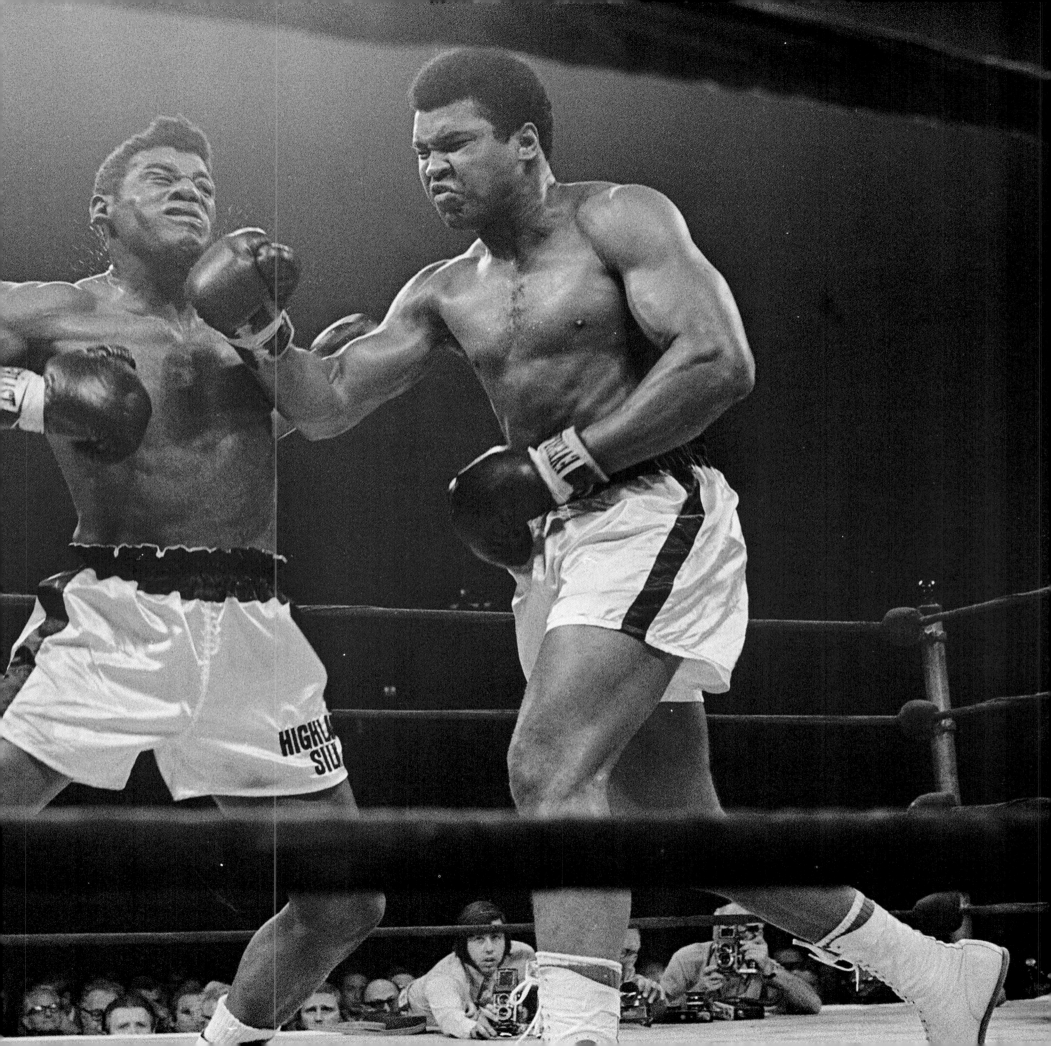

ever, from Ali, who had promised to crawl across the ring if Frazier won. 'You the champ,' said Ali, as they embraced each other. 'We don't do no crawling,' replied Frazier. 'We both bad niggers — we don't do no crawling.'

The end for Ali? Or was it? Would he truly surrender or did he have it in him to surmount this new challenge, to regain his title? It was to take him three-and-a-half painful, frustrating years, the same length of his exile, to find the answer, to prove he truly was The Greatest, and his mettle was tested every step of the way, especially by Ken Norton. Ali returned to the ring four months after the worst night of his life to beat his old pal and sparring partner Jimmy Ellis with a twelfth-round stoppage. Then followed a succession of comeback fights, including a one-sided seventh-round stoppage against Quarry in which Ali virtually begged the referee to halt the slaughter. Then came an equally fatuous match against Patterson which was also concluded in the same round.

Britain's Joe Bugner, an Adonis-like, Hungarian-born heavyweight, was next, but though he traveled the full 12 rounds, he hardly pushed Ali all night. The next test, supposedly another warm-up, came in the form of Norton, but it was far from that. Norton, a top-tenner who had hardly set the scene alight, bemused Ali with his crossed-arms style and shattered him in the second round with a punishing right that broke his jaw. Ali was in agony and Dundee begged him to quit. But such was the great man's make-up that he insisted on soldiering on, only to lose a 12-round points decision. It was courage of the highest order but did Ali little good because he was confined to hospital to have the misshapen jaw wired up.

Now was the time to quit, surely, because, for the second time in two years, his invincibility had been shattered. But Ali was unmoved. He was convinced his

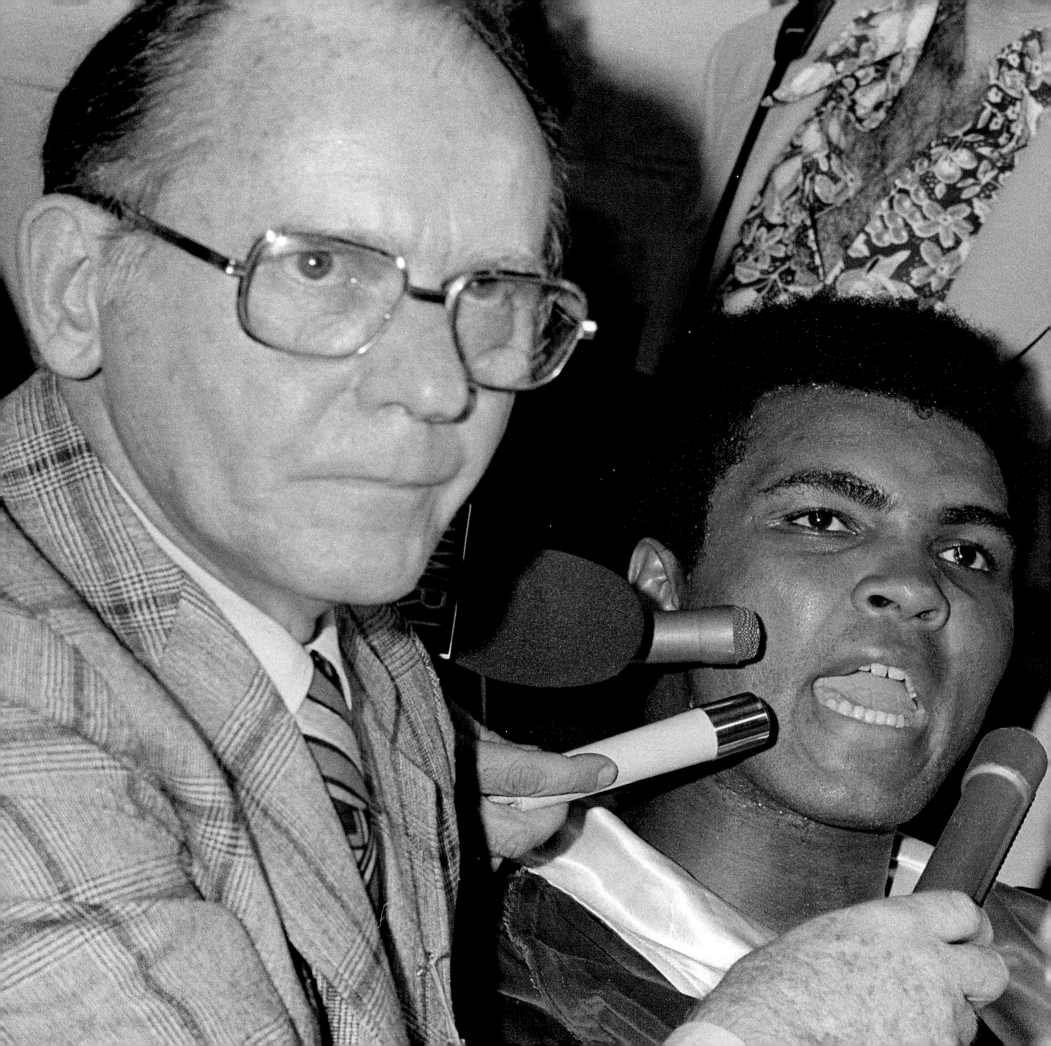

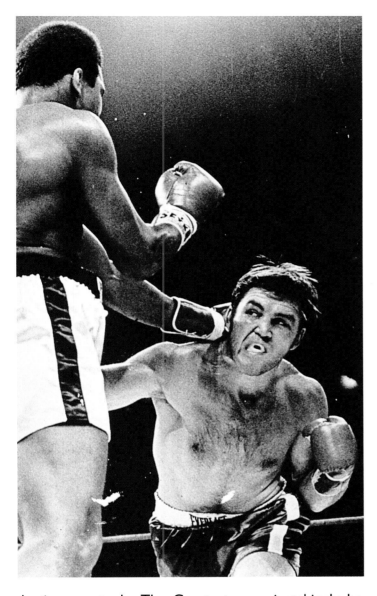

Left: 10 May, 1973, Philadelphia. Muhammad Ali now thirty-one years old still aiming for the heavyweight title as he shows his left fist to the camera during an interview in Philadelphia.

Center Left: 27 June, 1973. Muhammad Ali vs Jerry Quarry. The fight was stopped by the referee after 7 rounds.

Far Left: 28 September, 1972. Muhammad Ali faces reporters after his fight with Floyd Patterson.

destiny was to be The Greatest so, painstakingly, he began rebuilding his career yet again. His first exam, much against Dundee's wishes, was with the dangerous Norton. By this time George Foreman had hammered Frazier in two rounds to take the world title and his handlers knew there was only one pot of gold to look forward to — a showdown with Ali.

Ali had other things on his mind first, like revenge over Norton, and he stressed that Foreman and everyone else would have to wait. His chance came five months later, after his wired-up jaw, and his heart,

had mended and, although he had to make do with a points win, at least he had avenged a sorry defeat. Ali went looking for more revenge three months later when he tackled Frazier and, with his old speed of foot back in evidence, beat him comfortably in a 12-round eliminator in New York. 'I've evened up two old scores and wiped out the bad taste of defeat,' said Ali. 'Now I'm thinking about retirement, about a life with my family and children.' But the decline was finally over and there was one more goal: the world championship. Ali was aiming for the stars yet again.

the
SECOND COMING

JUST THREE MONTHS
OFF HIS THIRTY–THIRD BIRTHDAY AND ALI WAS READY TO WAGE WAR

on Foreman, the Colossus who looked even more formidable than the Liston of old. Conversely, just as Cassius Clay was deemed too young to match Liston, so boxing's afficionados felt Ali had regressed too far and was too old to stand up to the new monster. But the old Louisville Lip was convinced that his superior all-round ability could negate Foreman's thunderous power-punching, which lifted poor Frazier clean off the canvas when he took the title from him.

Previous Page: Muhammad Ali in training for his fight against Al 'Blue' Lewis, Dublin, 1972.

Right: 30 October, 1974, Kinshasa, Zaire. Heavyweight Champ George Foreman, throws a left to the eye of Muhammed Ali during their title bout. This shot twisted Ali's face but not his direction.

Such was the worldwide impact of the fight that Ali's manager Herbert Muhammad, via astute American promoter Don King, was able to negotiate with Zaire, an emerging African nation formerly called the Belgium Congo, to stage the richest promotion in history with $12 million being promised to cover costs and both fighters guaranteed nearly 50 percent. It was the first time a government had ever sponsored a title fight and, thanks to King and Herbert, it certainly wouldn't be the last.

Both fighters planned to wind up their training in Kinshasa, where the fight was being staged, a fortnight before the event, and Ali pulled what he felt was a master stroke by employing among his sparring partners Bossman Jones, a light-heavyweight who had worked with Foreman for several weeks. What he told Ali when questioned extensively about the world champion, however, should have persuaded him not to tackle Foreman. In Ali's intriguing autobiography *The Greatest*, Bossman tells him chillingly: 'The people accept George as a brute and they come to see him knock somebody out. George got the guns to do it. I see fighters who could stun you, who could knock you out, but George is the first one I been in the ring with I know can kill you. He may never kill nobody and I hope he never does, but he's got the power to kill, and he knows it. He has a special punch called the "anywhere" punch because anywhere it hits you, it breaks something inside you — a muscle, a bone, a shoulder, a finger, a rib.'

Bossman painted a formidable picture of the champion and when Ali asked about his weaknesses, Jones replied, 'He ain't got none.' When Ali asked if Bossman ever tagged him in training, Jones said: 'The sparring partners know better than to hit him. Once you hit him he'll tear your head off.' He also warned Ali that he couldn't get away with fighting on the ropes, as he had done in recent years: 'George knows how to

Next Page: 30 October, 1974, Kinshasa, Zaire. George Foreman looks up from flat on his back after Muhammad Ali knocks him down in the 8th round.

93

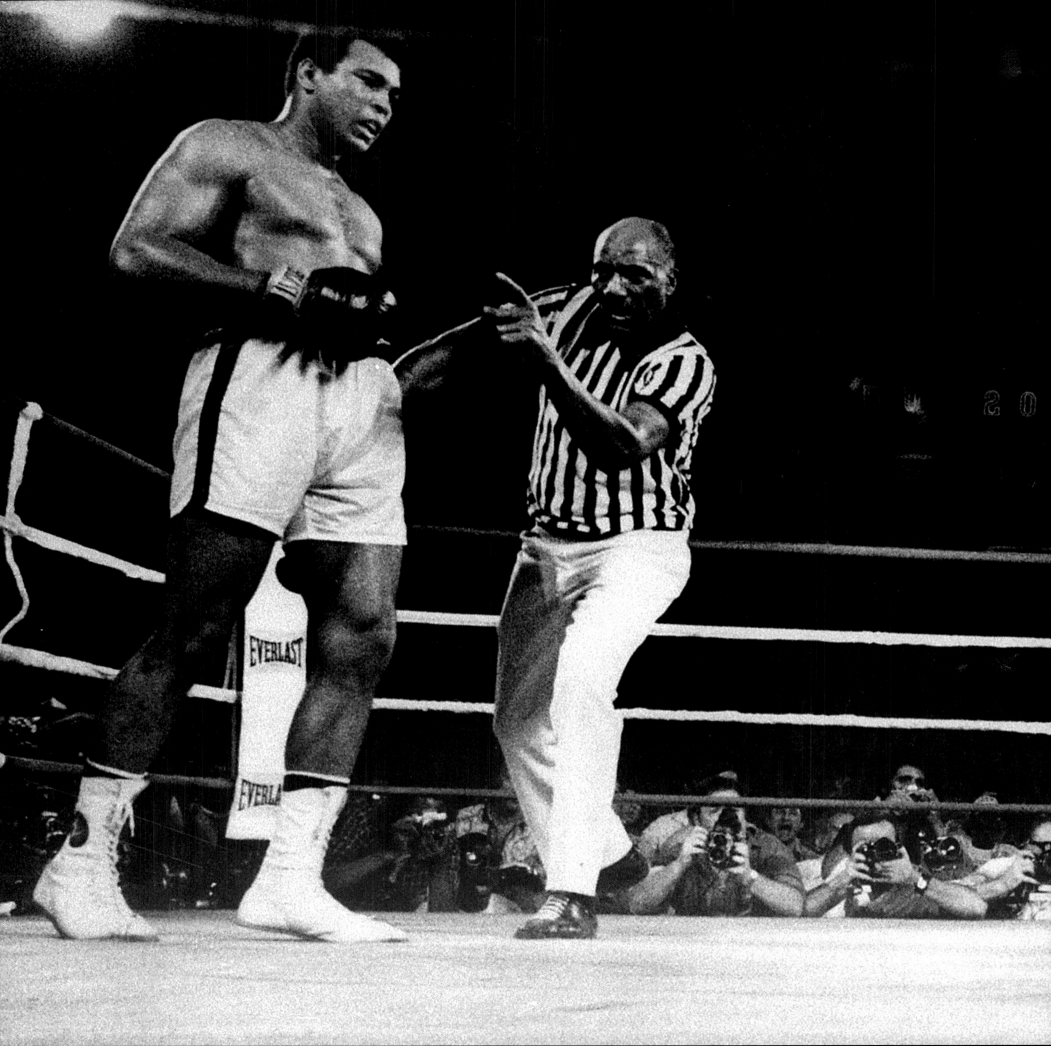

corner a man and he can lift you up off your feet with one punch. If you lay on the ropes and rest, he's gonna break your ribs. He'll hit you on your way down or on your way up. By the time the referee gets there you might be beat to death. His most killing punch is a kidney punch. That's the only part of the body you can't tighten up.' As if to compound the enormous task facing Ali, Bossman added: 'George wants to win this fight bad. He wants to be accepted by the world as the real heavyweight champion. It's killing him. It's eating him up to have the title and have them still call Muhammed Ali, the People's Champion.'

For all that, Ali remained cocksure that his superior strategy would suffice. . . but then came a bombshell. With days to go before their showdown, Foreman sustained a nasty freak cut above his right eye, caught accidentally by an elbow while sparring. Ali's heart sank because he knew this would be his only chance to tackle Foreman. Fortunately Dick Sadler, Foreman's trainer, was an expert 'cuts' man and managed to seal the wound without the need for stitches. Two weeks later he was back in the ring sparring, his eye completely healed, and at 3.45am (9pm in New York) on his 55th day in Zaire, Ali stepped out to the greatest reception of his life. As he made his way to the ring for his date with destiny, the huge moonlit crowd began chanting 'Ali, Ali Bom a ye, Ali, Ali, Bom a ye'(it came out as 'boom ah yea' and meant 'Knock him down, kill him dead'). Ali danced around the ring, getting the feel of it and waving to the excited crowd. They loved him, loved his showmanship, and while Foreman failed to appear for fully 10 minutes, Ali used the time wisely, keeping warm and whipping up a crescendo of support.

When Foreman did arrive he stood, arms raised in the center of the ring, his massive frame silhouetted against the sky. He looked what he was: an absolute monster.

Left: Foreman and Ali exchange blows during their bout for the World Heavyweight Championship.

Yet when the referee Zack Clayton called them together to administer the usual instructions, there was little to choose between their physiques. Ali was in magnificent shape for the greatest challenge of his life. He needed to be because right from the start he discovered Foreman was a lot smarter than he had given him credit for. When he started dancing to put space between them, Foreman cut the ring off with mammoth strides. He had been brilliantly schooled by old Archie Moore and Ali realized within a minute that his original stick-and-run plan just wouldn't work. 'I was having to take six steps to his two; and I realized I would be worn out long before him,' said Ali afterwards. Immediately he revised the plan and went against everything Bossman had warned him of by staying on the ropes. True, it was painful, almost pitiful to watch, as Foreman thundered in blows from all angles, especially into his body. Ali covered as best he could and indeed negated many of them with his arms, but it was inevitable some would get through, and they did toward the latter stages of the opening round.

Dundee pleaded with Ali to stay off the ropes during the interval, but he didn't know what Ali knew. 'I felt George's power and I knew why he had destroyed Frazier and Norton,' he said. Again in *The Greatest* Ali recalls vividly: 'My cornermen are screaming and I hear friends at ringside pleading for me to move out off the ropes, I taunt George, I goad him. "You ain't got no punch, you phony. Show me something, sucker," George roars in like a mob. He's throwing punches with tonnage I never thought a fist could carry. A crowbar in George's right hand crashes through my guard into my head, knocks me into the room of half-dream. My head vibrates like a tuning fork. Neon lights flash on and off. I've been here before. . . George's blows explode into my kidneys, my ribs, my head. I lean back, I slip and slide. I catch some on my arms, off

Far Left: 1973. Muhammad Ali throws a punch at Ken Norton during one of their two bouts in this year.

Left: 25 January, 1974, New York. Muhammad Ali vs. Joe Frazier. Ali won after 12 rounds.

my elbows, but I stay on the ropes. . . then near the end of the round I rise up and shoot quick, straight jabs and right crosses directly into George's head. POW! POW! POW! And I keep talking. I must not let him think his blows can stop me talking. "Sucker, is that all you got. Is that the hardest you can hit?"'

Ali was aware Foreman had forecast he would wipe him out in the third round the first time he'd had to travel that far in years — but he hung on through the biggest pounding he was ever to experience.

Right: 2 December, 1974,
London. Muhammad Ali lifted
by weightlifter Precious
McKenzie.

Far Right: January, 1974. A
portrait of Muhammad Ali as
he trains in the ring at his
training camp.

'Every punch is a haymaker, I block them from my head and suddenly he switches, comes up from the floor with an uppercut that seems to blow my jaw off. I'm hurt, I try to hold on. I try to move off but he pushes me back like a rag doll. The tuning fork in my head is humming. I've got to hold on, got to keep him from following up. George senses I'm hurt and he's coming in for the kill. I block, move back and weave. It's the longest round I've ever fought in my life, but near the end my head begins to clear ... suddenly I come out from under with straight lefts and rights directly into his face. WHAM! WHAM! WHAM! They're not powerful but they shake him up. George looks startled. He throws his heaviest bomb. It curls around my head and we clinch so tight I feel his heart pounding. I bite his ear. "Is that the best you can do, sucker? Is that all you got, Chump? You in big trouble, boy!"'

Foreman had every right to feel confused as he went back to his corner because no one had ever stood up to an assault like that, let alone emerged from such a shelling to fight back. But Ali wasn't just anybody. He was The Greatest, The Bravest of All, and, as the crowd applauded his courage, screeching 'Ali, Ali, Bom a ye,' he knew he was getting to Foreman. But there was much pain and suffering to come yet. Through the next four rounds he allowed Foreman to pound away on the ropes, springing to life at the end of each one to remind the monster of the size of his heart. Round by round the enormous exertions began to take their toll on the champion. The punches, though still awesome, came slower, more ponderous as his arms grew weary, and his breathing was heavier. But the fierce pace had also shattered Ali and he knew he would have to finish it quickly before Foreman got his second wind. Into the eighth round of this most punishing fight and in his mind Ali thought to himself. 'He LOOKS like King Kong but does he have the

Right: Ali holds a 'Wanted' poster of himself at his training camp.

heart of a lion, a Joe Louis, a Rocky Marciano, the heart of a Joe Frazier?'

The answer was swift in coming. Foreman pawed out a left and, with lightning reactions, Ali responded with a right over the top, then a mighty straight right to the jaw. Almost in slow-motion, King Kong's eyes became glazed and just as slowly he crumpled to the canvas. At eight he rose and was back on his feet even as the ref reached 10. But it was too

late. The greatest fighter in history had just won the 'Rumble in the jungle.' 'Ali proved his greatness time and again, not least in Kinshasa,' says Harry Mullan, Editor of Britain's weekly magazine *Boxing News*. 'He was six different fighters in one because he had the unique ability to adapt to every situation, to whatever obstacle was put in his way.'

Ali should have retired then and there, surrounded by thousands of adoring fans, but he just couldn't. He

Left: 24 May, 1976, Munich.
Ali vs. Richard Dunn. Ali pre-
vailed in the 5th round with a
knockout.

loved being champion again, loved being called 'Champ.' Three defenses in as many months followed, the first against no-hoper Chuck Wepner just five months after his finest hour. Wepner should have been a pushover and Ali treated him as such, and got a tremendous shock when his 'rope-a-dope' bum of the month actually floored him. It was deemed a push but Wepner, bleeding profusely from cut eyes and mouth, kept coming back for more. Finally, he succumbed in the fifteenth round of a real battering. At the ringside in Cleveland that night was a young actor named Sylvester Stallone, a committed boxing fan who was full of admiration for Wepner's bravery. It gave him an idea, and the character 'Rocky' was born. The rest, as they say, is history.

Ali defended against Ron Lyle, a tough ex-convict, then Britain's Joe Bugner, before the inevitable third and final show-down with Frazier. If Ali had gone to

the gates of Hell and back in dismantling Foreman, then he surely entered Hades in the rubber match with his arch-enemy. He labeled it the 'Thrilla in Manila,' another great deal worked out with a nation's government for megabucks, and Ali freely admitted that he wanted to quit the fight at the end of the tenth round, such was the pain in his belly from Frazier's relentless onslaught. But the champ had never before quit in his life, so the hurting went on and on.

**Far Right: 24 March, 1975,
Richfield. Ali stands over his
opponent, Chuck Wepner,
after knocking him down
against the ropes in the 15th
round of their championship
fight in Richfield.**

**Right: 17 June, 1975, Kuala
Lumpur, Malaysia. Ali takes a
break from a workout in the
National Stadium to address
spectators. He told the crowd
that he had a new defensive
tactic which he would use
against British challenger Joe
Bugner. The champ also said
he was 99 percent sure he'd
retire from the ring following
the bout.**

Something had to give because both men were
giving and taking far too much punishment and in the
end it was left to the fatherly figure of Eddie Futch,
Frazier's veteran handler, to wave the white flag of
surrender. 'You love a fighter like your own child,'
Futch was prone to say, and somehow you always felt
he meant it. He certainly did on an unbearably hot
night in the Philippines. With just three minutes to go
and with the by now non-Smokin' Joe arguing furious-
ly in his corner, Futch called over referee Carlos
Padilla and restored some sanity to the proceedings.

Frazier, his eyes mere slits gaping through huge
swellings, cried the tears of a loser. Ali, too exhausted
even to raise his arms in triumph, slumped to the floor
and was tended to by the same men who would later
throw him to the young lion called Larry Holmes, the
same Larry Holmes who as a 21-year-old had helped

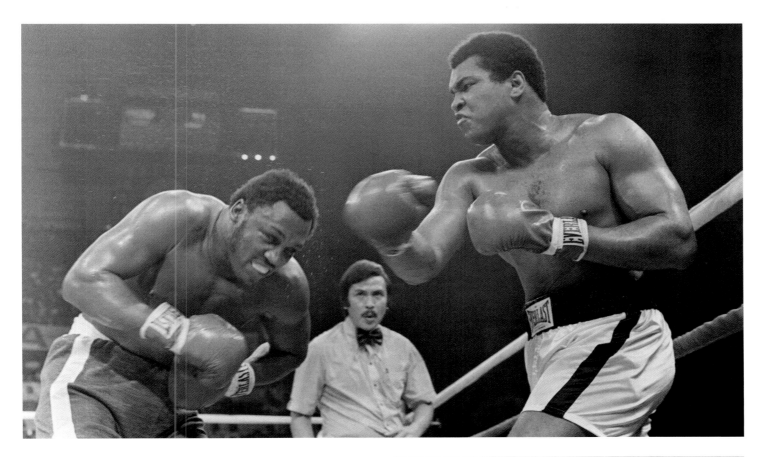

Far Left: 30 June, 1975, Merdeka Stadium, Kuala Lumpur. Muhammad Ali beat Joe Bugner on points.

Left: 30 September, 1975, Manila. Ali lands a right on challenger Joe Frazier's head, as referee Carlos Padilla, Jr. looks on during the 7th round.

Below Left: Ali punches Joe Frazier during their title bout.

him prepare for the Foreman fight. The fourteenth round was memorable, perhaps for all the wrong reasons. Frazier, arms by his side and his head resembling a football, took punch after punch but just refused to stop marching forward. Ali, at melting point but disguising it brilliantly, threw everything in his bid to end the torture. By the end of the round he had, but at a terrible price.

Afterwards, his voice barely audible, Ali confessed it was the closest thing to dying. And something did die that night: Ali's prime! It had been a brutal battle and Ali had again got himself into superb mental and physical condition. But he finished a 'shot' fighter. It should have been his last hurrah but pride, and the urgings of his confidants, said otherwise.

the DAY THE MUSIC DIED

THE LAST THING ALI

NEEDED WAS ANOTHER WAR, YET HE GOT ONE AGAINST BOGEY–MAN KEN NORTON. The ex-marine was No. 1 contender and his awkward style really troubled Ali. The venue for the match was the famous old Yankee Stadium and Norton had been fine-tuned by the wily Futch. After 15 torrid rounds, most observers were convinced they were seeing a new champion because Norton had boxed with aggression and guile. But Ali's immense reputation, plus his flashy finish to rounds, were enough to sway the decision his way. Just!

Futch and Norton were seething, claiming you had to KO the champion to get a points decision, and they weren't far wrong. It happened again against Jimmy Young, a light-punching, high-skilled Philadelphian who played the ageing Ali at his own game and floated like a butterfly all night. Ali was lucky to win a split-decision and, clearly, his grip on the world heavyweight scene was slipping fast. Yet he could still produce glimpses of the old magic, as he did against shaven-headed Earnie Shavers, one of the fiercest single-punch exponents ever. Ali neutralized all his early bombs at Madison Square Garden in 1977 to score a comprehensive points victory.

But a cat has only nine lives and Ali used the last one up that night. In his next defense the following year he took on seven-fight novice Leon Spinks, a crude yet game slugger whose claim to fame was an Olympic light-heavyweight gold in the 1976 Montreal Games. The gap-toothed challenger fought like a man possessed to outscore an under-prepared Ali, and not even the judges' sentiment could help him this time. But still Ali wasn't through and he returned fitter and sharper than for some time to deliver a boxing lesson against Spinks and become the first and only champion to win the heavyweight title three times. It was a perfect time for Ali to hang up his gloves, and it

seemed he had faded from the scene when his crown was vacated. But the lure of the dollar and the limelight proved too much and one fateful morning in 1980, Ali set off once more for the gymnasium to prepare for a comeback fight against a peak Larry Holmes.

By this time his second marriage had also failed and, after leaving Belinda with their four children, including Muhammad Ali Jnr., in 1975, he was wed to a beautiful model, Veronique Porche, who caused a scandal when she appeared in Manila for Ali's third Frazier fight three years earlier. At the age of 38 he should have been playing with those kids and enjoying the trappings of wealth instead of reaching for an elusive dream by punishing himself and his body still further. Yet many believed him when he said he could return to topple his old sparring partner, by now installed as World Champion.

As ever, he talked a magnificent fight and he certainly looked the part when he clambered into the ring with not an ounce of fat showing after months of training. This was the legend who had led Liston a merry dance, had withstood Foreman's mighty salvos and even forced Frazier to surrender. But it was all an illusion and a weight-drained Ali was a mere shell with nothing left inside. Many fights since boxing began have left a nasty taste in the mouth and this was one, a contest no true fan likes to remember. If the music died the day Buddy Holly crashed out of the sky, as Don Maclean proclaimed in song, then this was the night boxing wept genuine tears after Ali's 10-round humiliation.

Ali clowned right up to the first bell, but could do nothing as Holmes took him apart systematically. Even he must have been horrified at Ali's ineptitude, his total inability to muster up a combination, to defend, to even shuffle. Shamble more like. By the seventh Holmes, as ruthless as his nickname the 'Easton

Right: Muhammad Ali dances
as Japanese wrestler Antonio
Inoki tries a leg kick during
the 4th round of their
wrestling-boxing exhibition
fight. Ali fought to a draw with
Inoki.

Assassin' indicated, began pulling his punches for the first and only time in his glittering career. The ending, when it came, was as sickening as the fight itself, with Ali sitting mesmerized in the corner and Dundee and Bundini Brown arguing over whether the slaughter should be curtailed. Brown, unbelievably, wanted it to continue but Dundee's 'I'm the chief second and I'm stopping it' gave relieved referee Richard Greene the excuse he had been looking for to call a halt.

Amazingly, Ali was to fight yet again, losing on points to champion-to-be Trevor Berbick 13 months later. But on a cold, bleak Las Vegas night against Holmes, the Ali music died. The fans who streamed out of Caesar's Palace didn't say a thing. . . there was nothing left to say. Tragically, Ali, though still a regular at ringside and still a great crowd-puller, is a pitiful, shambling wreck of a man, committed to a life of drugs to combat the dreaded Parkinson's Disease as well, it must be said, as the accumulative effect of the needless wars he fought.

His third marriage also fell apart when Veronique began making progress in movies only for Ali to forbid her from doing love scenes. After seven years they divorced amicably with Veronique citing 'irreconcilable differences.' Next came Yolanda Williams, the girl next door in Louisville whom he'd known since childhood. But even that fourth marriage, in 1986, hit a depression when a former girlfriend who said she had a six-year-old love child through Ali, confessed to a four-day fling with him. It served to add to the general confusion about him, his career, his alleged excessive taste for women and his current health, which even today appears to hit highs and lows, with reports one day of revolutionary wonder drugs clearing his mind, and others of his complete mental disintegration.

Ali himself said recently: 'If I had to do it all over again I might have quit after losing to Spinks. But I

Above: 27 August, 1976, Washington D.C. Secretary of State Henry Kissiger and Muhammad Ali appear to be engaged in some serious negotiating at a reception. Both men attended the World Boxing Association awards dinner.

boxed on for three years. If God had wanted me to quit earlier I would have. There's a reason for everything and I have no regrets. You have to weigh good with bad and I've had a full life, experienced the lot. I have more peace of mind now than ever. Wish I could talk better, but the brain is alert. I've got more attuned to the things around me in the last few years. You know, like deaf people can maybe feel the ground rumbling, I'm like that.'

Would he have beaten, say, Mike Tyson, in his prime? Just watch the video of Cassius Clay whipping Liston, of Ali toppling Foreman. Watch his fight almost to the death against Frazier. He'd have beaten anyone.

Time and again Muhammad Ali proved he was The Greatest, the smartest. But it still wasn't enough for the warrior who transformed heavyweight boxing. He transcended the thud and blunder and gave us sheer poetry. If only he'd remembered his lines a little better.

Ali's marriage to Veronique Porche had yielded two daughters, Hana (1976) and Laila (1979), giving him the impressive total of eight children — seven girls and a boy. His relationship with fourth wife Yolanda, more commonly known as Lonnie and a graduate of Vanderbilt University who started cooking for him when he was sick, survived the revelation that he'd

Left: 29 September 1977. Earnie Shavers covers up during the first round of his match with Muhammad Ali.

strayed, and was cemented in 1991 when the couple adopted a son, Asaad. The contented trio retired to a life of relative seclusion on his farm in Berrien Springs, Michigan, where Ali — his mental faculties seemingly unimpaired — slowly came to terms with his physical problems.

But seclusion is almost impossible when you're one of the world's most recognizable figures. This became clear one afternoon in December 1991 when, while heading home in his Rolls-Royce, he passed a car with its bonnet raised; a group of college students gathered helplessly, their journey interrupted. Ali's arrival at the side of the road caused something of a stir, the

students (who'd not even been born as he hit his boxing heyday) standing in total awe as he untangled a set of jump leads he'd found in his car boot. He attempted to restart the stalled vehicle as passing vehicles honked their salute. One car even swerved out of the fast lane to stop, reverse and deliver a greeting: 'Ali, we love you! You are the greatest!' The three-time world heavyweight champion responded by blowing kisses.

Thankfully, the possibility of an accident was averted since, having failed in his attempt to get the stricken car started, he departed the scene with two students on board, having vowed to get them back to

campus. When one asked for an autograph, Ali simply signed a pamphlet on Islam and offered his cheek for a chaste kiss; on receiving it, he fell back as if poleaxed by a straight left before smiling a farewell.

One of Ali's past opponents made news again in October 1994. Jerry Quarry had faced Muhammad in the ring on two occasions, the first when he'd been the unfortunate man in the Atlanta ring in October 1970 when the former world title holder stormed back after being stripped of his crown. Despite lasting just three rounds on that occasion, Quarry faced Ali again in June 1972 when the fight was once more stopped, this time in the seventh. Though Ali had emerged the victor on both occasions, it was the

vanquished Quarry who showed compassion by forming a foundation to research the link between boxing and brain damage. Quarry's mission statement mentioned that three members of his family who had turned to professional boxing had suffered permanent disablement, but his former opponent was also clearly in his thoughts.

The pair had more in common than many realized. Quarry had exhibited signs of dementia as early as 1982, and a neuropsychologist who'd examined him later in the decade estimated that boxing had aged him by some 30 years. The name for his disorder was dementia pugilistica, the effects of which were exhibited through symptoms of the better-known

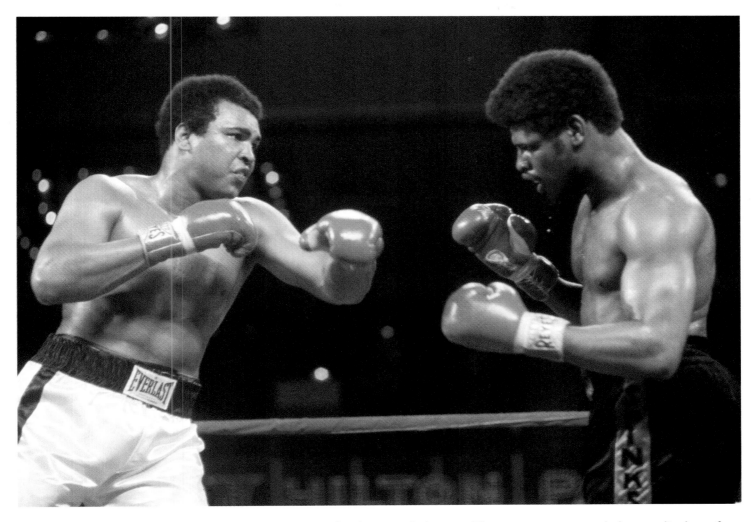

Parkinson's and Alzheimer's. Together, they cause both loss of memory and motor movement.

He spotlighted the lack of extensive research on this subject, plus the lack of a pension plan for permanently injured boxers — a crucial point, given that Quarry was surviving on benefits. Having fought on past the age it was safe to do so but unable to afford retirement, he'd pocketed just $1,050 for his final fight in 1992 in Colorado, a state where no boxing licence was required, compared with a $338,000 payday when facing Ali for the first time. 'My goals are to start a research program to learn more about how to treat and care for the injured athletes,' said Quarry. 'This would include a building or buying a facility for care

and therapy. The government and the medical profession also need to be educated on how to safeguard all sports to prevent brain damage. Maybe some day we will develop regular screening for all athletes who apply for an amateur or professional license to compete in contact sports.'

The foundation announced its intentions via news releases in sports magazines and newspapers worldwide, starting off by sponsoring charity events. It would not now be long, however, before Quarry's better-known and more successful opponent re-emerged in his own right.

If Muhammad Ali had been absent from the headlines for the best part of a decade since his illness was

Right: Muhammad Ali has a solemn look as he sits in his corner and hears that he lost his heavyweight title to Leon Spinks by a split decision.

Far Right: Ali starts right to the head of challenger Leon Spinks in the 7th round.

Right: United Nations Secretary-General Kurt Waldheim accepts one of two 'paintings for peace' from and executed by Muhammad Ali. The works of art, to be on permanent display at the UN, were presented in honor of the Year of the Child.

diagnosed, then 1996 would go down as the year that put him right back on the media map. It was suitable, too, that this was to happen at the Olympic Games, the event where, back in 1960 in Rome, he'd stolen the limelight as young light-heavyweight Cassius Clay.

His triumph then had been tempered with sorrow. Legend had it he'd thrown the hard-won medal into the Ohio river after being refused service at a diner, declaring 'I was the champion of the Olympics, the man with the gold medal... and it didn't mean nuthin'.' Nevertheless, the following years had seen him build

a legend on that first successful step on the world stage. The pain of rejection had encouraged him to fight for his beliefs as hard as he fought for sporting honours, rejecting his slave name and challenging the prejudice inherent in American society. And it was for this as much as his ring record that he was remembered.

The athletes from 197 countries who gathered in Atlanta's Olympic Stadium had earlier recalled another son of the South, civil rights campaigner Dr. Martin Luther King. His widow Coretta was in attendance

and she, along with her son Dexter, had helped carry the Olympic torch on its way to the opening ceremony. King's legendary 'I have a dream' speech from 1963 rang out once again through the gathering gloom. King had died while striving for his vision that black and white could live together in harmony, but the world was soon to recall that another legend who'd fought for human rights was still with us, albeit with abilities impaired.

The stadium stood shrouded in darkness as the Centennial Games awaited the lighting of the ceremonial flame. Yet the identity of the athlete deputed to do the deed was the best kept secret of the opening ceremony. The choice was Muhammad Ali, the most distinguished athlete the closing century had produced — his task to use the torch delivered, as was the custom, by a team of runners linking the venue with Greece where the games had their birth. And it was altogether appropriate that, as the TV cameras first caught sight of the man bringing the flame into the arena, he was identified as Evander Holyfield, the former world heavyweight boxing champion and an Atlanta resident.

From Holyfield, the torch was passed to Greek hurdler Paraskevi Patoulidou, from the country when it all began, then four-times gold medal swimmer Janet Evans, representing the USA. As she mounted the podium and stood before the site of the flame, she

Far Left: Ali with a very young fan.

Left: Talking with a fan at his training camp.

Below Left: 15 September 1978, New Orleans. Ali slams a right hand into the face of Leon Spinks, sending a shower of water from Spinks head.

was joined by the familiar figure of Ali, whose sudden, unexpected appearance drew huge and delighted applause. He acknowledged this by holding the torch high in his right hand; only his trembling left betrayed the physical handicap under which he labored.

The stadium — not to mention a worldwide TV audience estimated at 3.5 billion — held its collective breath as the former champion fumbled with the torch, almost doing the unthinkable and dropping it. His target was a taper that ran up to the top of a tower to ignite the Olympic flame that would burn brightly throughout the Games 'I kept touching it,' he said later, 'the whole world was watching. . . and the damn thing won't light.' Then, all at once, the flame flared into life, signifying the start of the games and the audience, including a teary-eyed President Clinton, clapped sympathetically as Ali was ushered away. Muhammad Ali had another golden memory to put alongside his medal win in his scrapbook.

Later in the week, the International Olympic Committee awarded Ali a replica medal to replace the one he'd thrown away in disgust all those years ago. The ceremony took place during the half-time interval of the basketball final between the US Dream Team and Yugoslavia, the medal presented by IOC president Juan Antonio Samaranch. As a man, the 35,000-strong crowd rose to their feet to cheer, an ovation acknowledged by the man known simply as 'The Greatest' by solemnly raising both arms in the air.

A straight-faced and apparently unmoved Ali kissed the IOC president on both cheeks, then kissed the medal — but when the Dream Team players engulfed him a familiar smile of delight emerged. 'He's a role model for a lot of our guys,' said Dream Team player Reggie Miller. 'To be in arm's reach (of him) was very special.'

The games' opening ceremony had clearly been special to Ali, too — indeed, he was still clutching the torch when taken back to his hotel suite. Refusing to loosen his hold on the now-charred firebrand, he sat silently in an armchair for several hours, deep in thought and re-running who knows what memories. 'I think he was just completely awed by the whole experience,' Lonnie Ali recalled. 'He found it very hard to come back down to earth. There was just such a fabulous response. No one expected that.'

The symbolism of a flame was to play a pivotal role in his next crusade — a campaign to eradicate Parkinson's Disease. Called 'Blazing Towards A Cure,' it was launched in Washington DC late that September, and by reprising his Atlanta performance and lighting the first 'Fighting Flame' Ali set in motion a worldwide campaign based around the National Parkinson Federation's 45 Centers of Excellence, all of which lit similar beacons.

Interestingly, there had been just one dissenting voice of criticism as Muhammad Ali re-lit his own personal flame. It came from Joe Frazier, the man who'd been first to dent the champion's unbeaten record back in 1971, only to lose out himself three years later. Frazier was reported to have said that Ali was 'a draft dodger who didn't like his white brothers or his black brothers,' insisting that, as a man in good physical condition, he would have been a better choice 'to run all the way up there and light the flame.'

The Olympic flame had certainly restored Muhammad Ali's profile; as demand for his presence grew, figures of $100,000 for a day and $225,000 for overseas trips were being mentioned. Celebrated US magazine *Sports Illustrated* featured him on their cover, while the year of 1996 would end with a similar cover feature in *Vanity Fair*. For this he was photographed by celebrity snapper Annie Leibovitz.

Sport and showbiz have always been close relations, but for Ali this was never more so than when, in March 1997, an Academy Award was awarded to the

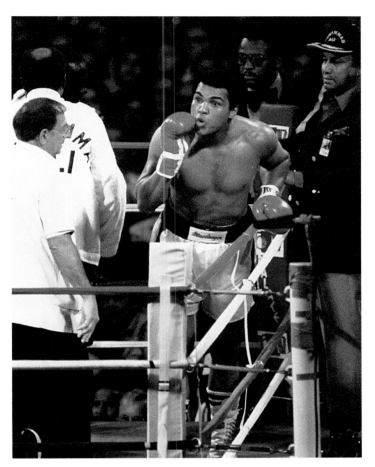

Far Left: 2 October, 1980. Muhammad Ali vs. Larry Holmes. Ali's final bid for the title ended in disaster.

Left: Ali in training for his fight with Larry Holmes, October, 1980.

Below Left: Ali vs. Holmes Ceasars Palace, 1980. Ali was forced to retire in the 11th round.

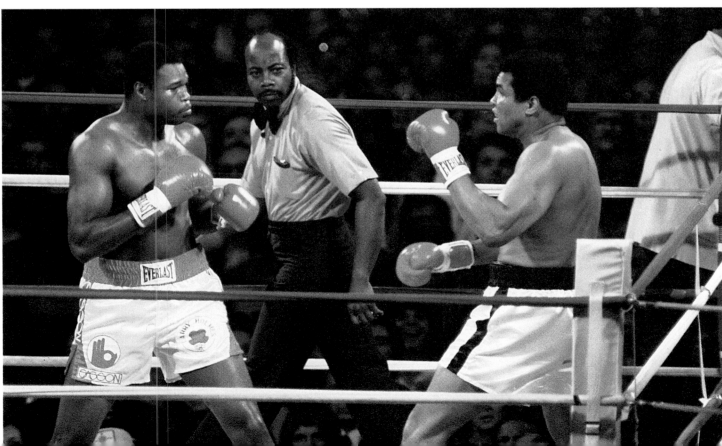

Left: 17 July, 1980, New York. In what has become the classic clowning confrontation known popularly as fight signing, Muhammad Ali pokes his fist at Larry Holmes, while promoter Don King keeps them apart. The show was to announce a heavyweight title bout between the two in Las Vegas.

Right: Larry Holmes and Muhammad Ali trade blows during their heavyweight championship bout at Caesars Palace.

Far Right: 2 February, 1981, New York. Jack Dempsey takes a poke at Muhammad Ali during the first Thurman Award Dinner of the Association for the Help of Retarded Children. The award was presented to Dempsey, Ali, Billy Martin, Senator Bill Bradley, Ralph Kiner, Cliff Robertson, Ethel Kennedy and Munson's widow, Diana.

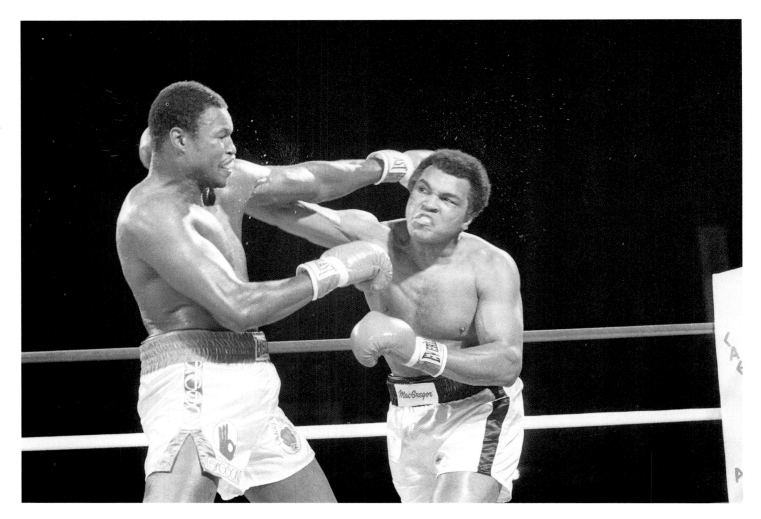

documentary film *When We Were Kings*. This could justly claim to have been longer in the making than almost any other celluloid documentary — but the results, by common consent, were spectacular. Director Leon Gast had filmed Ali and Foreman's title fight in Zaire back in 1974, but had lacked the funds to complete it. In point of fact, he'd intended to cover a three-day pop concert that preceded the fight, but this flopped when the match was delayed six weeks due to Foreman sustaining a cut when sparring.

Gast must have been glad he stuck around. To add to the sense of perspective, he intercut contributions by the likes of Spike Lee, biographer Thomas Hauser and other contemporary 1990s figures to leaven the

ringside commentary by Norman Miler and George Plimpton. Don King was in evidence, having extorted a $10 million purse from Zaire's President Mobutu.

But the real star was Ali, who had started playing mind games with favorite Foreman long before they reached the ring. An early press conference saw Ali come out with the classic line 'I'm so mean I make medicine sick.' And with time on his hands due to Foreman's injury, he continued to weight the psychological scales until they were very much in his favor. Ali clearly won the crown outside the ring as much as the 27 minutes he spent in it.

The film's producer David Sonenberg paid him a warm tribute. Muhammad Ali, he said, was 'more than

Far Left: 1981, New York. Muhammad Ali gestures during a news conference at which he said he would hit the comeback trail. Ali, 39, said, 'I want that fourth title.'

Left: 1983, New York. Muhammad Ali and his wife, Veronica, chat with author Norman Mailer at a bash marking the 50th anniversary of *Esquire* magazine at Lincoln Center's Avery Fisher Hall.

just an athlete. He had the charisma, grace, intelligence, vocabulary and chutzpah and it was clear that he had an agenda that went way beyond just merely knocking people on their asses.'

Even before the Oscar for Best Documentary Feature was awarded — Ali and Foreman taking the stage together to a standing ovation — a proposed full-scale bio-pic appeared on the horizon. Actor Mykelti Wilkinson was the man in the frame after winning rave reviews for his appearance in *Forrest Gump*, and the sponsor HBO (Home Box Office), which had

previously used Ali in their 'Beyond The Ring' community service program. The actor's agent confirmed that the two had already been in contact. 'They've talked, and even sparred,' she revealed, adding that Ali 'loves Mykelti' and would be happy to be played by him.

Williamson had received a letter from the ex-champion, she continued, 'and he said he was happy to see that Mykelti's choice of roles were good portrayals of black Americans. Then I got them together and it dawned on everybody just how similar they were.'

**Right: Muhammad Ali, 1985.
His legend and glory have not
faded with retirement from
thr ring.**

Left: New York, 1986. Muhammad Ali and Joe DiMaggio stand side by side after receiving Liberty Medals at Ellis Island.

Someone who also fancied playing the young Ali was actor-pop singer Will Smith. The *Independence Day* star was reported to be lined up as lead in a $30 million Warner Bros epic, with Jon (*Batman*) Peters producing. The project had been in development for nearly ten years, with Oliver Stone lined up at one point to direct, and if true the skinny Smith would have to put on an estimated 40 pounds for the role.

It was perhaps surprising that Smith hadn't been lined up in a singing capacity to appear at an October benefit concert in Los Angeles for the Muhammad Ali World Healing Project — but he wasn't missed from a bill boasting the likes of Prince and Celine Dion. 'I wish people would love everybody else the way they loved me,' commented Ali, who went on to explain his aim of raising money for existing charities working to combat prejudice and bigotry.

Right: 1984. Friends Muhammad Ali and Sylvester Stallone play boxing.

Though Muhammad Ali had opened his professional career in his home town of Louisville in 1960, his last fight there had been in November 1961, when he'd knocked out Willi Bosmanoff in the seventh round. Just short of 36 years later, he returned to the ring in Louisville for three one-minute rounds of 'mock boxing' for a charitable donation of $50,000.

The pageant in September 1997 was to celebrate the first year of the Ali Cup, an international amateur competition which attracted 96 competitors from fully 30 countries. 'We hope this great event will put Louisville on the map as a center for boxing,' commented mayor Jerry Abramson. Indeed, the Cup won

instant official backing when it was announced its results would determine the members of the US boxing team at the following month's World Championship in Hungary. Another welcome spin-off was the raising of some $1 million to go towards a museum and education center in Louisville to bear Ali's name.

The Ali Cup festivities were also notable for the presence of several other former heavyweight champions, notably Jimmy Ellis, Ken Norton, Evander Holyfield and Mike Tyson. The latter pair were no strangers, having met a mere matter of months earlier when Tyson had left the ring in disgrace after

Left: Two great boxers with The Greatest — Joe Frazier, George Foreman and Muhammad Ali.

biting off a chunk of his opponent's ear. They had responded to Ali's invitation in the hope that the incident — which cost Tyson £3 million and his boxing licence, revoked for a year — could be put formally in the past. Holyfield's statement read: 'The meeting is a great way to cleanse the sport of boxing of an incident we all regret.'

Ali's sporting exploits — not to mention his courage in returning to the public gaze — were recognized in 1997 by the Arthur Ashe Award for Courage. He was the fifth person to receive the accolade named after the late, great Afro-American tennis player, to whom Ali paid the following tribute:

'My admiration and love for the man is boundless. He was a man of vision, compassion and courage, and I only hope the legacy I leave on this earth is as rich and meaningful as his has been.'

Legacies of course can be material as well as spiritual, and news of a sporting auction of Ali's boxing memorabilia was to be held in Los Angeles in October brought a quick reaction from his camp. 'Muhammad wants the public to know that he is not endorsing and not participating in this auction, nor has he provided any items,' said a spokesperson, while the man himself added 'Over the years people around me took things. . . I want all my stuff!'

The 3,000 objects up for sale included his 1960 Golden Gloves trophy (which would reach $25,000) and a letter he'd written to the Draft Board requesting a new classification, sent just before he refused induction into the armed services ($55,000). Some of the articles had been stored at his father's Louisville home and apparently sold without Ali's approval, but he refused to condemn those who'd buy, saying only 'It means they love me.'

In the end, the auction house compromised and agreed to send a letter to all purchasers asking if they'd consider selling or lending the item to a proposed Muhammad Ali Center in Louisville. A portion of the total $1.3 million raised was also donated to the Muhammad Ali World Healing Project. Top price was paid for the robe, trunks and boots Ali wore in the 1974 'Rumble in the Jungle.' The white calf-length robe decorated with African patterns and elaborate beadwork fetched $140,000 — an auction record for boxing memorabilia — while the trunks ($50,000) and boots ($52,000) went to separate bidders. Fascinatingly, too, the robe included a silk handkerchief sewn into its lining with an astrologer's written prediction of an Ali win!

In January 1998, the soccer teams of Morocco and Angola were the ones seeking victory as they faced each other in Casablanca, and Ali was present in an 80,000-strong audience. His appearance on the pitch all but overshadowed the home side's 2-1 victory, but the stakes were somewhat higher two months later

Left: 20 September, 1984, New York. Ali was hospitalized because of Parkinson's syndrome but declared that he's still The Greatest. Ali met with reporters outside the hospital with his friend of 20 years, the Reverend Jesse Jackson. Before entering the hospital, Jackson called Ali a 'hero for our generation.'

when he attended a committee of the House of Representatives in Washington DC. The purpose was to ensure Parkinson's won its fair share of funds — $100 million being the target figure — as consideration was given to the research needs of various wasting diseases. The committee paid tribute to Ali as he sat silent and trembling, adding 'You bring us all hope.' Congress passed the bill, but an accounting dispute with the National Institute of Health seemed likely to lower the actual amount allocated.

The same month, *Time* magazine had invited one of the century's most famous faces to grace its 75th anniversary gala at Radio City Music Hall in New York along with Presidents Clinton and Gorbachev and fellow sportsmen including Joe DiMaggio and tennis ace

Donald Budge. But for Muhammad Ali the serious business of fund-raising always took precedence over such galas, wife Lonnie as ever by his side to do his speaking for him. 'It's amazing the number of people I come across on a daily basis who are being afflicted,' she said at one of the many rallies they attended. 'I've been told a cure for Parkinson's is simply a function of money.'

In August came a report that Ali was to try a new treatment method at the South Florida town of Boca Raton. Retired dentist Jerry Jacobson claimed a 'resonance machine' he'd invented could cure the former heavyweight champ by means of a weak magnetic field. Ali received his treatment sitting between two magnetic eight-foot high circles in a garden chair,

Jacobson claiming that the magnetic waves would stimulate 'homeotic genes' that normally turn off after childhood and these would cause cells in Ali's brain to regenerate. The cells would then produce dopamine, a deficiency of which causes Parkinson's. 'I've been to 15 different doctors,' Ali said, explaining his willingness to be a guinea pig, 'and none of them have been able to do anything.'

At least 135 patients would have to participate for the Food and Drug Administration to take Jacobsen's claim seriously; he believed it to be effective on everything from osteoarthritis in the knee to neurological disorders. Ali's participation certainly brought him the oxygen of publicity, as in a smaller way did fellow sports celebrities Dave Davis (bowling) and Doug Tewell (golf) who sought relief from knee and elbow pain, but for Ali at least the association was to end in tears. He would quit the program in March 1999, saying he felt his privacy had not been respected. 'I feel I was used to promote their clinic,' Ali complained in a statement, while Jacobson responded, perhaps somewhat naively: 'I feel really awful. . . it's just that the media came on too strong.'

Meanwhile, Muhammad continued his philanthropic work. His aim to supply four million free meals to hungry children in Canada bore fruit in the summer of 1998 thanks to fund-raising concerts by soul legends Ben E. King and Gary U.S. Bonds, while September saw medical supplies delivered to Cuba. He spent three days there with Lou Grant TV star Ed Asner delivering $1.2 million in aid and meeting with President Fidel Castro. This was in defiance of the long-standing US economic embargo on Cuba originally intended to overthrow communism and restore democracy.

November brought sadness — the death at 91 of promoter Chris Dundee, brother of Ali's legendary trainer Angelo — but also happier news: confirmation from viewers of TV channel ESPN2 that Muhammad Ali was still The Greatest. He received nearly four times as many votes from visitors to the channel's website than did runner-up Sugar Ray Robinson. Ali paid this tribute: 'I'm honored, but there were many who went before me who paved the way. My idol will always be Sugar Ray Robinson, who was, and remains, one of the best pound-for-pound fighters to have ever lived in this century.'

Ali's influence on black culture was reinforced by an article in *GQ* magazine focusing on various aspects of his life. 'Ali — the Poet' was written by Darryl McDaniels of top rap group Run-DMC, who reminisced about his childhood in Queens, New York, when he and his friends would pretend to be Muhammad Ali after seeing his televised fights. 'No-one had enough money to buy real boxing gloves, so we'd take our parents' puffy ski gloves. . . and we'd set up a makeshift ring. You wanted to be either Bruce Lee or Muhammad Ali.' He emphasised the fact that the Louisville Lip's legacy lived on with rap groups like his own. 'Usually you'd see an interview with a boxer and he could barely talk. But Ali was fluent in English in a way we hadn't seen. His speech was sweet, and it had a melody; he almost sang when he spoke. "Float like butterfly, sting like a bee." Those words were the most famous rap lyrics ever. Ali was a spokesman, a messenger, a prophet, a representative, a diplomat and an ambassador. He was a king.' McDaniels' payoff was both profound and perceptive. 'Though he is quiet now, he is speaking louder than ever.'

Ali himself was no stranger to profundity, having authored a book with friend Thomas Hauser, called *Healing*. Its creation was inspired by Ali's habit of writing down phrases from books, most notably the Koran, that moved him. Hauser had chosen the title

Left: 1985, Muhammad Ali and Hulk Hogan holding Liberace.

Below Left: 1985. A pensive Muhammad Ali in the boxing ring once again.

Right: 1988. Muhammad Ali and Jack Nicholson.

when he found A-L-I jumping out of the middle of the word H-E-A-L-I-N-G.

By late 1998, Will Smith's place in the Ali bio-pic seemed to be assured, with Barry Sonnenfeld lined up to direct a film with the title *Power And Grace*. Smith saw his future role as helping him combine elements of comedy, action and drama. 'It would be a combination of Robin Williams, Eddie Murphy and Arnold Schwarzenegger.' And, though it wasn't the first time Ali had appeared to endorse a young actor, an appearance in Smith's video for the hit single 'Just The Two Of

Us' with one of his daughters suggested there might be some truth in the rumor.

Also in October, the Muhammad Ali Center in Louisville opened its doors, Governor Patton doing the honors. It had been founded at the second time of asking, and was an attempt by the local boy made good to give something back to the community from which he'd taken on the world — and won. Ironically, just before this new facility bearing his name opened, Ali had sold his training camp to a former aide, George Dillman. He purchased the six-acre site for

Left: 1986 Olympic Games, Atlanta, Georgia.

Below Right: 1996. Sylvester Stallone, Muhammad Ali, Riddick Bowe, Michael Buffer, Sugar Ray Leonard, Lennox Lewis, Vinny Pazienza, and Carl Weathers clench fists at a Rocky anniversary celebration at the All Star Café.

Below Left: 29 August, 1996. Ali speaks with First Lady Hillary Clinton, who sits in her box with daughter Chelsea at the 1996 Democratic National Convention.

Right: 1996. Sylvester Stallone
and Muhammad Ali at a
Rocky anniversary celebration
at the All Star Café.

Far Right: August 1996. Ali and
model Iman promote the
*Muhammad Ali: The Whole
Story* film documentary at
Essex House.

the same price Ali had asked 17 years earlier, when Dillman hadn't had the money to complete the deal. Ali had developed the Deer Lake camp in 1972, and trained there until his final fight against Trevor Berbick in 1981. It would now become a bed and breakfast establishment. . . albeit one with many fascinating sights for fight fans.

Among the mementoes of its former owner inside the gym were hooks for the punch-bags he would pummel and a screen on which he would project film footage of past boxing greats, as well as forthcoming opponents. One of the log cabins, painted white with a minaret-style roof, was where Ali knelt every day to pray while facing Mecca. Indeed, Ali continued to devote time each day to reading the Koran, a habit which became a part of his life in 1964 when he changed his name from Cassius Clay.

The new year of 1999 opened with the sad death of Jerry Quarry, who'd fought Ali twice back in the early 1970s and whose foundation had shown such farsightedness in calling for research into boxing and brain disease. He was just 53, and the cause of death was the same dementia pugilistica, (brain damage caused by repeated blows to the head) that he had sought to research five years earlier .

It was a timely reminder that no-one knew how much boxing contributed to health problems in later life. March would find Ali lobbying for a bill sponsored by Senate Commerce Committee chairman John McCain that would protect boxers from exploitation and give them more of a say in their own destiny. 'Professional boxers have, for too long, been the target of unscrupulous managers and promoters,' he said. At the same time, he added his voice to many who claimed that the recent title fight between Evander Holyfield and Lennox Lewis had cheapened the heavyweight division and boxing in general, calling Holyfield's disputed point victory 'the biggest fix in fight history.' The sport, he said, 'had sunk to its lowest levels.'

The fact that Muhammad Ali remained a man whose opinion counted was underlined in February when his feats were commemorated on the most unusual location to date. . . a breakfast cereal box! 'My career demonstrates that everyone should follow their dreams,' he said. 'Growing up in Louisville, it would have been difficult to believe that I would win the heavyweight title three times. Now, I'm honored that Wheaties has chosen to recognize me with my own box.'

Left: 12 June, 1997. Boxing promoter Don King poses with Ali. This was taken at a party to celebrate King's induction into the International Boxing Hall of Fame.

Below Left: September 1997. Former heavyweight boxer Ken Norton talks with Muhammad Ali during the Muhammad Ali Tribute celebration.

Below Right: Don King with wife Henrietta and Muhammad Ali during the party to celebrate King's induction into the International Boxing Hall of Fame.

The 12-ounce special-edition 'Ali Wheaties' box was an appropriate best-seller in what was designated national Black History month. And if that didn't impress young fans, then the donation of his personal ring to the Dowagiac Boxing Club in Michigan just might have. The just-opened club aimed to keep teenagers off the streets and out of trouble by supplying both physical and mental stimulation, and delighted owner Larry Seurynck felt Ali's boxing ring would be a 'vehicle to reach people.'

Reaching people was what Muhammad Ali was all about — and touching them not with his boxing glove

Right: Ali stands next to
Evander Holyfield as he
speaks at the Muhammad Ali
Tribute.

Far Right: Ali attends the Mike
Tyson hearing, Clark County,
Las Vegas.

but his presence and spirituality. When he came to
London in February 1999, fight fans with long memories harked back to June 1963 and his historic
Wembley meeting with Henry Cooper, not to
mention his two fights within three months in 1966
when first Cooper and then Brian London felt the
power of his flailing fists. But three decades and
more had passed since then, and people with that kind
of recall were thin on the ground. Fans, though,
weren't. Amazingly, thousands too young to have seen
Ali fight were flocking to touch the hem of his
metaphorical garment.

His arrival in Britain in February 1999 was at the
behest of Irish rock singer Bono. The frontman of U2
was a big enough name in his own right to hog the
headlines, and he was preparing to use the Brits —
the British record industry's annual awards show – as
his platform. But Bono (real name Paul Hewson) was
shrewd enough to realize there was someone he
could call upon whose image and resonance spread
far beyond even his own.

The cause was a new one, but no less noble than
Ali's quest for a cure for Parkinson's. Jubilee 2000, as
the campaign was dubbed, was an attempt to get

developed nations to cancel Third World debt by the
end of the first year of the next millennium. The Pope,
the Dalai Lama and Archbishop Desmond Tutu were
among Ali's fellow patrons, but only one had graced
the occasion with his presence. Muhammad's
introduction from the stage led to familiar chants of
'Ali, Ali,' but it was only the following day when he
left the company of the music-biz fat cats and took
to the streets of London that the real Ali effect
was apparent.

The purpose was to visit the Lambeth Refugee
Resource and Development Centre, where the Jubilee
2000 campaign was to be opened. This was situated in
Brixton, a population center of Londoners of Afro-
Caribbean descent, but admirers of every size, color
and creed were visible thronging the streets as the
champion passed slowly through them in an open-
topped Bentley limousine.

Jubilee 2000 director Ann Pettifor explained that
Ali's appointment as their international ambassador
was because 'He is an icon for all people who have
struggled against the inhumanity of racism and war. He
carries his scars and his achievements with tremendous dignity.' That dignity, she continued, was 'shared

Left: The Ali tribute featuring
Evander Holyfield.

by the millions in Africa, Latin America and Asia who daily struggle against the economic, human and social degradation caused by debt.' Certainly Ali's world travels on humanitarian causes had given him first-hand experience of that.

True to the multi-cultural nature of the event, Ali wore a pullover knitted in different colours as he held children in his arms, signed autographs and pressed the flesh. Next came a series of familiar magic tricks as he made a red handkerchief vanish before getting down to business. On arrival at the center, he signed his most important autograph of the day when he added his name to Jubilee 2000's petition. Then he

went into closed session with the leaders of the campaign, accompanied by his agent and lawyer Ron DiNicola. Apparently, those who were privileged enough to participate were awed by his presence; when a speaker put across the point that the objective was to bring freedom to the countries shackled by debt, Ali rose to his feet, all eyes upon him. . . only to silently punch the air with his fist in a victory gesture. The room erupted. . .

Earlier that day, he had joined half a dozen children to lay wreaths of remembrance at a monument in Westminster, Central London. The children were symbolic of the young lives that could be saved if Third

World countries could use their money for investment rather than paying off paper debts to the developed world — an estimated seven million lives were at stake by the end of the year 2000. After a one-minute silence, Ron DiNicola expressed Ali's gratitude at his reception in words.

'It's a terrific honor for Muhammad to be in a country he loves and one he's had a warm and long-standing relationship with. He has had a long-standing commitment to the people of Africa and the other poor countries of the world, and it's an honor for him to be here in support of such a worthy cause.'

Those who met Ali were suitably impressed. Campaign co-ordinator Kofi Mawuli Klu said that he had 'lifted our spirits by identifying himself with this campaign because he only fights just causes,' adding that the former champion had already 'changed the world for many black people by what he did in the ring.' Similarly, Toure Moussa Zeguen, who'd fled to Britain from the Ivory Coast, was hopeful Ali's inter-

Left: September 1997.
Evander Holyfield speaks at
the Muhammad Ali Tribute.

vention would bring the campaign closer to its goal. 'It will take the G8 (developed) countries to cancel the debts,' he said after meeting his hero, 'but Ali has made us believe it can happen.'

Though he enjoyed the love and adulation of millions, thanks largely to using his public image for good in the latter half of the 1990s, Muhammad Ali also derived great pleasure from time spent on his farm in Berrien Springs with his nearest and dearest. Washington Post staff writer David Maraniss was offered a rare glimpse of The Greatest on home turf in summer 1997, and reported a man with much more going for him than many had thought.

'His disorder. . . is not as debilitating as one might suspect from catching a brief glimpse of him,' said Maraniss. 'He is agile enough to dress himself each morning. He knots his ties perfectly. He lifts his legs to put on his socks. Laces his shoes. Slips on his Swiss Army watch. Feeds himself. Opens doors. Performs magic tricks. Reads his Bibles and Korans. Writes

Right: April 1997. Ali walks
with his wife, Lonnie, at the
Essence Awards.

Far Right Above: 26
September, 1998. Ali in
Melbourne, Australia.

Far Right Below: 16 January,
1999. Ali sits next to his
daughter Leila during the
Mike Tyson and Francois
Botha fight at the MGM
Grand Garden Arena in Las
Vegas. Tyson won the fight
after a KO in the 5th round.

legibly. Talks on the telephone. Understands every-thing said to him and around him. Flips the remote on his television to watch CNN and Biography and the Discovery Channel.'

A contemplative Ali revealed to Maraniss that he was contemplating his forthcoming 'House in Heaven.' Explaining he could make a 'hundred dollars a picture' signing autographs, he said that, now he wasn't fighting any more, he signed them for nothing. 'Get the money, give it to the homeless . . . Give it to soup lines if I see someone who needs some. Here's a hundred. Here's fifty. Soup vendor. Wino. Old woman with varicose

veins. Good deeds. . . Whatever colour you are, no matter how much money you have — politics, sports — you're gonna die.' Life, he concluded, was 'A test. Trying to pass the test. I'm trying. . .'

As the millennium approached, Muhammad Ali con-tinued to travel the world, spending an average of 275 days a year on the road meeting presidents, monarchs, religious leaders and the common man. The torch had yet to splutter and die: the flame still burned in the soul of the man they called The Greatest.

Left: January 1988. Muhammad Ali in the Tournament of Roses Parade.

Next Page: 1996. Muhammad Ali receives an honorary gold medal from Samaranch, the President of the International Olympic Committee at the 1996 Olympic Games.

MUHAMMAD ALI'S
FIGHT RECORD

Muhammad Ali's FIGHT RECORD

DATE	OPPONENT	VENUE	RESULT ROUND	

1960

DATE	OPPONENT	VENUE	RESULT ROUND	
29 OCTOBER	Tunney Hunsaker	LOUISVILLE, KENTUCKY	**W** 6	
27 DECEMBER	Herb Siler	MIAMI BEACH, FLORIDA	**W KO** 4	

1961

DATE	OPPONENT	VENUE	RESULT ROUND	
17 JANUARY	Tony Esperti	MIAMI BEACH	**W KO** 3	
7 FEBRUARY	Jim Robinson	MIAMI BEACH	**W KO** 1	
21 FEBRUARY	Donnie Fleeman	MIAMI BEACH	**W KO** 7	
19 APRIL	Jim Robinson	LOUISVILLE	**W KO** 2	
26 JUNE	Tony Esperti	LAS VEGAS, NEVADA	**W** 10	
22 JULY	Jim Robinson	LOUISVILLE	**W** 10	
7 OCTOBER	Tony Esperti	LOUISVILLE	**W KO** 6	
29 NOVEMBER	Jim Robinson	LOUISVILLE	**W KO** 7	

1962

DATE	OPPONENT	VENUE	RESULT ROUND	
10 FEBRUARY	Sonny Banks	NEW YORK	**W KO** 4	
28 FEBRUARY	Don Warner	MIAMI BEACH	**W KO** 4	
23 APRIL	George Logan	LOS ANGELES, CALIFORNIA	**W KO** 4	
19 MAY	Billy Daniels	NEW YORK	**W KO** 7	
20 JULY	Alejandro Lavorrante	LOS ANGELES	**W KO** 5	
15 NOVEMBER	Archie Moore	LOS ANGELES	**W KO** 4	

1963

DATE	OPPONENT	VENUE	RESULT ROUND	
24 JANUARY	Charlie Powell	PITTSBURGH, PENNSYLVANIA	**W KO** 3	
13 MARCH	Doug Jones	NEW YORK	**W KO** 7	
18 JUNE	Henry Cooper	WEMBLEY, LONDON	**W rsf** 5	

1964

DATE	OPPONENT	VENUE	RESULT ROUND	
25 FEBRUARY	Sonny Liston	MIAMI	**W rtd** 7	WON WORLD HEAVYWEIGHT TITLE

1965

DATE	OPPONENT	VENUE	RESULT ROUND	
25 MAY	Sonny Liston	LEWISTON, MAINE	**W KO** 1	RETAINED WORLD TITLE
22 NOVEMBER	Floyd Patterson	LAS VEGAS	**W rsf** 12	RETAINED WORLD TITLE

1966

29 MARCH	George Chuvalo	TORONTO, CANADA	**W** 15	RETAINED WORLD TITLE
21 MAY	Henry Cooper	HIGHBURY, LONDON	**W rsf** 6	RETAINED WORLD TITLE
6 AUGUST	Brian London	LONDON	**W KO** 3	RETAINED WORLD TITLE
10 SEPTEMBER	Karl Mildenberger	FRANKFURT, WEST GERMANY	**W KO** 12	RETAINED WORLD TITLE
14 NOVEMBER	Cleveland Williams	HOUSTON, TEXAS	**W KO** 3	RETAINED WORLD TITLE

1967

6 FEBRUARY	Ernie Terrell	HOUSTON	**W** 15	RETAINED WORLD TITLE
22 MARCH	Zora Folley	NEW YORK	**W KO** 7	RETAINED WORLD TITLE

EXILED FROM APRIL 1967 TO SEPTEMBER 1970 AND STRIPPED OF WORLD TITLE

1970

26 OCTOBER	Jerry Quarry	ATLANTA, GEORGIA	**W rsf** 3	
7 DECEMBER	Oscar Bonavena	NEW YORK	**W KO** 15	

1971

8 MARCH	Joe Frazier	NEW YORK	**L** 15	
26 JULY	Jimmy Ellis	HOUSTON	**W KO** 12	
17 NOVEMBER	Buster Mathis	HOUSTON	**W** 10	
26 DECEMBER	Jurgen Blin	ZURICH, SWITZERLAND	**W KO** 7	

1972

I APRIL	Mac Foster	TOKYO	W 15	
I MAY	George Chuvalo	VANCOUVER, CANADA	W 12	
27 JUNE	Jerry Quarry	LAS VEGAS	W rsf 7	
19 JULY	Al 'Blue' Lewis	DUBLIN, IRELAND	W KO 11	
20 SEPTEMBER	Floyd Patterson	NEW YORK	W rsf 7	
21 NOVEMBER	Bob Foster	LAKE TAHOE, NEVADA	W KO 8	

1973

14 FEBRUARY	Joe Bugner	LAS VEGAS	W 12	
31 MARCH	Ken Norton	SAN DIEGO, CALIFORNIA	L 12	
10 SEPTEMBER	Ken Norton	LOS ANGELES, CALIFORNIA	W 12	
20 OCTOBER	Rudi Lubbers	JAKARTA, INDONESIA	W 12	

1974

| 28 JANUARY | Joe Frazier | NEW YORK | W 12 | |
| 30 OCTOBER | George Foreman | KINSHASA, ZAIRE | W KO 8 | REGAINED WORLD TITLE |

1975

24 MARCH	Chuck Wepner	CLEVELAND, OHIO	W KO 15	RETAINED WORLD TITLE
16 MAY	Ron Lyle	LAS VEGAS	W KO 11	RETAINED WORLD TITLE
30 JUNE	Joe Bugner	KUALA LUMPUR, MALAYSIA	W 15	RETAINED WORLD TITLE
30 SEPTEMBER	Joe Frazier	MANILA, PHILIPPINES	W rtd 14	RETAINED WORLD TITLE

1976

20 FEBRUARY	Jean Pierre Coopman	SAN JUAN, MEXICO	W KO 5	RETAINED WORLD TITLE
30 APRIL	Jimmy Young	LANDOVER	W 15	RETAINED WORLD TITLE
24 MAY	Richard Dunn	MUNICH, WEST GERMANY	W KO 5	RETAINED WORLD TITLE
28 SEPTEMBER	Ken Norton	NEW YORK	W 15	RETAINED WORLD TITLE

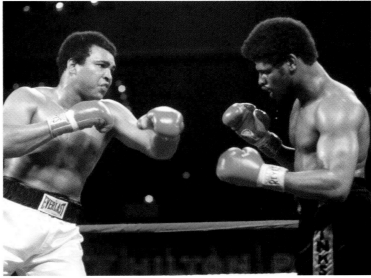

1977				
16 MAY	Alfredo Evangelista	LANDOVER	**W** 15	RETAINED WORLD TITLE
29 SEPTEMBER	Earnie Shavers	NEW YORK	**W** 15	RETAINED WORLD TITLE
1978				
15 FEBRUARY	Leon Spinks	LAS VEGAS	**L** 15	LOST WORLD TITLE
15 SEPTEMBER	Leon Spinks	NEW ORLEANS, LOUISIANA	**W** 15	REGAINED WORLD TITLE
1979				
	ANNOUNCED RETIREMENT			
1980				
2 OCTOBER	Larry Holmes	LAS VEGAS	**L rtd** 11	FOR WORLD TITLE
1981				
11 DECEMBER	Trevor Berbick	NASSAU, BAHAMAS	**L** 10	

INDEX

Left: 1980, Las Vegas. Muhammadi Ali vs. Larry Holmes, Press Conference.

CREDITS

ACKNOWLEDGEMENTS

The publisher wishes to thank all the picture libraries and photographers who supplied the illustrations for this book. The photographs on the following pages were kindly provided by:

Corbis/Bettmann for pages 2, 10, 11, 12, 14, 16, 19, 20, 22-23, 24-25, 27, 28-29, 31, 32, 33, 34-35, 38-39, 40, 41, 42-43, 45, 46 (both), 47, 51, 52, 53, 54, 55, 56, 57, 58-59 (both), 60-61 (both), 65, 66, 67, 68, 69-70 (both), 72, 73, 74, 76-77, 79, 80, 81, 84-85, 86-87, 88, 89 (right), 92-93, 94-95, 96-97, 104-105 (both), 106-107 (both), 109 (both), 112, 113, 114-115, 116-117, 118, 119, 121, 122 (all), 125 (bottom), 128-129, 130, 131, 132, 133, 136, 138, 139, 154, 155 (left and middle), 156 (both) and 157 (both)

Allsport/MSI for pages 7, 13, 63 (bottom), 75, 82-83 and 100

Corbis/Charles Harris; Pittsburgh Courier for pages 8-9 and 37

Allsport for pages 15, 91, 99, 120 and 123

Corbis/Hulton-Deutsch Collection for front cover and pages 17 and 48-49

Allsport/Hulton Deutsch for pages 50, 62, 63 (top), 64, 89 (left), 108 and 155 (right)

Corbis/Jerry Cooke for page 98

Corbis/Michael Brennan for back cover and pages 101, 102, 111, 124, 125 (top left and right), 145 (all), 146 (left), 149 and 150 (bottom right)

Allsport/Tony Duffy for page 103

Allsport/Steve Powell for pages 127 (all) and 159

Corbis/David Rubinger for page 134

Corbis/Joseph Sohm; ChromoSohm, Inc. for page 135

Allsport/Gray Mortimore for page 137

Corbis for page 141 (top)

Corbis/Lynn Goldsmith for pages 141 (bottom) and 142

Allsport/Michael Cooper for page 143 (top)

Corbis/Wally McNamee for page 143 (bottom left)

Corbis/Mitchell Gerber for pages 143 (bottom right), 144 (both) and 150 (left)

Allsport/Harry How for page 146 (right)

Allsport/Andy Lyons for page 147

Allsport Australia/Jack Atley for pages 148 and 150 (top right)

Corbis/Neil Rabinowitz for page 151

Corbis/Ales Fevzer for pages 153